D1250808

Baking Is Fun

Volume 6

Recipes 434-513

Cover Recipe Page 36

ISBN 0-9691357-5-0

Printed and Bound in Canada

Dear Readers:

Through travel, television and magazines we have all been able to learn about other places, people, their customs and traditions.

As North Americans or Australians we are fortunate to have a rich heritage of culture from people around the world, who have settled on this continent. Some of the recipes in this book may be familiar to you from your own family's background.

For our culinary trip around the world we have selected baking recipes from Austria to Australia and China to Sicily.

Recipes here include some which reflect typical country cooking through to the more sophisticated gateaux and tortes. You will discover recipes for appetizers from Russia and tiny deep fried Morsels from Spain.

Each recipe carries its own piece of history: Alexander Torte reminds us of Czar Alexander I; Hunyade Torte recalls the Hungarian commander-in-chief. There is a touch of the French finesse in the profiteroles and the Turkish sunshine in the Baklava.

In these recipes we have held the original concept to retain the authenticity of the recipe, while at the same time adapting them to North American cooking techniques.

We hope that these recipes will give you glimpses of other cultures, and by trying a specialty from another country, put you in the mood to plan your next vacation.

If you have any recipe ideas we are always pleased to hear from our readers.

Enjoy your voyage around the world of great baking recipes.

The following baking books are also available:
Baking Is Fun Volume 1, Recipes 1-93
Baking Is Fun Volume 2, Recipes 94-190
Baking Is Fun Volume 3, Recipes 191-270
Baking Is Fun Volume 4, Recipes 271-350
Baking Is Fun Volume 5, Recipes 351-433

You may order each of these books from

oetker Recipe Service
2229 Drew Road
Mississauga, Ontario
L5S 1E5

Contents

CAKES WIT

AMOUS NAMES

Recipe No. 434 Switzerla

Engadine Tart

Dough:

350	all-purpose flour	2⅓	cups
130 g	sugar	⅔	cup
pinch	salt		pinch
5 drops	**oetker** lemon flavouring concentrate	5	drops
1	egg	1	
150 g	butter or margarine, cold	¾	cup

Filling:

250 g	sugar	1¼	cups
50 mL	liquid honey	3	tbsp.
250 mL	whipping cream	1	cup
300 g	chopped walnuts	3	cups
45 mL	sherry	3	tbsp.

Glaze:

1	egg yolk, slightly beaten	1	
15 mL	milk	1	tbsp.

Dough:
PREHEAT oven to 200°C (400°F). Grease a 24 cm (9½″) springform pan.
SIFT flour onto pastry board. Make a well in centre
PUT sugar, salt, flavouring concentrate and egg in well. Work a little flour into centre mixture to make stiff dough.
CUT butter into small pieces over mixture.
WORK all ingredients together quickly to make a smooth dough.
CHILL slightly for easy rolling, about 30 minutes.
DIVIDE dough into 3 equal portions.
PRESS or roll ⅓ of dough onto base of prepared pa
SHAPE ⅓ of dough into a long roll. Press around inside rim of pan forming 4 cm (1½″) sides. Press seams to seal.
Filling:
HEAT sugar and honey together until melted.
ADD whipping cream and nuts. Mix well.
HEAT mixture. Let cool.
ADD sherry.
SPREAD filling evenly over dough.
ROLL out remaining dough. Cut into strips.
PLACE in criss-cross fashion over filling.
COMBINE beaten egg yolk and milk.
BRUSH over strips.
BAKE on middle oven rack at 200°C (400°F) for 35 minutes.
SERVE warm or cool.

Recipe No. 435 Isra

Jewish Chocolate Torte

Batter:

5	egg yolks	5	
120 g	icing sugar, sifted	1	cup
1 pkg	**oetker** vanilla sugar	1	pkg.
pinch	salt		pinch
40 g	cocoa, sifted	½	cup
80 g	ground hazelnuts	¾	cup
100 g	dry breadcrumbs	1	cup
5	egg whites	5	

Glaze:

50 g	shortening	¼	cup
30 g	cocoa, sifted	⅓	cup
100 g	icing sugar, sifted	¾	cup
45 mL	hot water	3	tbsp.

Decoration:

100 g	semi-sweet chocolate, shaved	4	sq.

Batter:
PREHEAT oven to 180°C (350°F). Grease a 25 cm (10″) springform pan.
COMBINE egg yolks, icing sugar, vanilla sugar and salt in mixer bowl.
BEAT at medium speed until light and fluffy.
SPRINKLE cocoa, hazelnuts and breadcrumbs over egg yolk mixture. Fold in gently.
BEAT egg whites to stiff peaks.
FOLD into egg yolk mixture, gently but thoroughly.
TURN batter into prepared pan.
BAKE on middle oven rack at 180°C (350°F) for 35-40 minutes.
REMOVE from pan and let cool.
Glaze:
COMBINE shortening, cocoa, icing sugar and water top of double boiler. Place over simmering water, stirring constantly until smooth.
SPREAD evenly over torte.
DECORATE with shaved chocolate.

Alexander Torte

Dough:

200 g	all-purpose flour	1⅓ cup	
½ pkg	**oetker** baking powder (7 g/1½ tsp.)	½ pkg.	
200 g	ground almonds	2 cups	
150 g	sugar	¾ cup	
1 pkg	**oetker** vanilla sugar	1 pkg.	
2 mL	ground cloves	½ tsp.	
2 mL	ground cinnamon	½ tsp.	
pinch	salt	pinch	
½ btl	**oetker** lemon flavouring concentrate	½ btl.	
1	egg	1	
200 g	butter or margarine, cold	1 cup	

Filling:

250 mL	whipping cream	1 cup
1 pkg	**oetker** Whip-it	1 pkg.
50 g	icing sugar, sifted	½ cup
45 mL	raspberry liqueur	3 tbsp.
300 g	strained raspberry jam	1½ cups

Decoration:

fresh whole strawberries or raspberries

Dough:
PREHEAT oven to 220°C (425°F). Grease a 22 cm (8½″) springform pan.
SIFT flour and baking powder onto pastry board. Make a well in centre.
PUT ground almonds, sugar, vanilla sugar, spices, sa flavouring concentrate and egg in well. Work a little flour into centre mixture.
CUT cold butter into small pieces over flour mixture
WORK all ingredients together quickly to make a smooth dough. Chill for easy rolling (1 hour).
DIVIDE dough into 4 equal portions.
PRESS or roll each portion, one at a time, onto base of prepared pan. Bake individually at 220°C (425°F) for 10-15 minutes.
REMOVE from pan and let cool.
Filling:
BEAT whipping cream to soft peaks. Gradually add Whip-it, icing sugar and raspberry liqueur, beating tc stiff peaks.
COVER each cake layer with jam. Put layers togeth
SPREAD sides and top of cake with ⅔ of whipped cream mixture.
PLACE remaining mixture in decorator bag and decorate torte attractively.
TOP with fresh strawberries or raspberries.

Portuguese Apple Torte

Dough:

300 g	all-purpose flour	2 cups
10 mL	**oetker** baking powder	2 tsp.
100 g	sugar	½ cup
1 pkg.	**oetker** vanilla sugar	1 pkg.
1	egg	1
120 g	butter or margarine, cold	½ cup

Filling:

600 g	apples	1⅓ lbs.
250 mL	port wine	1 cup
80 g	sugar	⅓ cup
100 g	raisins	1 cup
100 g	chopped almonds	1 cup

Decoration:

1	egg white, slightly beaten	1
	icing sugar, sifted	

Dough:
PREHEAT oven to 220°C (425°F). Grease a 24 cm (9½″) springform pan.
SIFT flour and baking powder onto pastry board. Make a well in centre. Put sugar, vanilla sugar and e in well. Work a little flour into centre mixture to ma a stiff dough.
CUT cold butter into small pieces over mixture.
WORK all ingredients together quickly to make a smooth dough. Chill for easy rolling, (30 minutes).
DIVIDE dough into 3 equal portions.
PRESS or roll ⅓ of dough onto base of prepared pan.
SHAPE ⅓ of dough into a long roll. Press around inside rim of pan forming 4 cm (1½″) sides. Press seams to seal.
Filling:
PEEL and core apples. Cut into small pieces.
COMBINE wine and sugar.
STEAM apples in wine mixture for about 5 minutes.
ADD raisins and almonds. Mix well. Cool.
SPREAD filling evenly over dough.
ROLL out remaining dough. Place over filling. Press sides together to seal. Brush with egg white.
BAKE on middle oven rack at 220°C (425°F) for 30-35 minutes.
SERVE warm or cool. Sprinkle with icing sugar.

Tarte Tatin

Pastry:

1 pkg	frozen puff pastry (397 g/14 oz.)	1 pkg.
Filling:		
100 g	sugar	½ cup
700 g	apples	1½ lbs.
30 g	butter or margarine, melted	2 tbsp.
1 pkg	**oetker** vanilla sugar	1 pkg.
5 mL	ground cinnamon	1 tsp.

Method:
THAW puff pastry according to package directions.
PREHEAT oven to 180°C (350°F). Grease a 24 cm (9½") springform pan and sprinkle with ½ of sugar.
PEEL and core apples. Cut into thick slices.
PLACE apple slices attractively in bottom of springform pan.
DRIZZLE melted butter over apples.
COMBINE remaining sugar, vanilla sugar and cinnamon.
SPRINKLE sugar mixture over apples.
ROLL out pastry into 26 cm (10") diameter round.
PLACE pastry over apples. With fork make several holes in pastry for air vents.
BAKE on middle oven rack at 180°C (350°F) for 45-55 minutes.
COOL slightly. Turn upside down onto serving plate.
SERVE warm.

Recipe No. 439 Ameri

Double Heart Torte

Batter:

5	egg yolks	5
120 g	sugar	¾ cup
30 mL	hot water	2 tbsp.
¼ btl	**oetker** lemon flavouring concentrate	¼ btl.
15 mL	rum	1 tbsp.
½ pkg	**oetker** baking powder (7 g/2 tsp.)	½ pkg.
30 g	cocoa	⅓ cup
50 g	semi-sweet chocolate, grated	2 sq.
5	egg whites	5

Filling:

1 pkg	**oetker** chocolate pudding powder	1 pkg.
100 g	sugar	½ cup
250 mL	milk	1 cup
30 g	semi-sweet chocolate, grated	1 sq.
150 g	sweet (unsalted) butter, softened	¾ cup
125 mL	whipping cream	½ cup

Decoration:

30 g	icing sugar, sifted	¼ cup
20 g	cocoa, sifted	¼ cup
60 g	sliced almonds, toasted	½ cup

Batter:
PREHEAT oven to 200°C (400°F). Grease a double heart-shaped springform pan.
CREAM egg yolks, ⅔ of sugar and hot water togethe on high speed of electric mixer until thick and cream Gradually add flavouring concentrate and rum.
COMBINE baking powder, cocoa and chocolate. Ad to creamed mixture. Mix well.
BEAT egg whites and remaining ⅓ of sugar to stiff peaks.
GENTLY fold egg whites into creamed mixture.
TURN batter into prepared pan.
BAKE on middle oven rack at 200°C (400°F) for 30 minutes.
REMOVE from pan immediately and cool completel
SLICE cake with thread to make two layers.
Filling:
PREPARE pudding according to package directions, using 100 g (½ cup) sugar. Stir in grated chocolate.
COOL to room temperature, stirring occasionally.
CREAM butter. Beat in pudding 1 spoonful at a tim (Butter and pudding must be at the same temperatur to prevent curdling).
BEAT whipping cream to stiff peaks. Reserve a little for decoration. Fold gently into pudding mixture.
SPREAD ⅔ of pudding mixture on bottom cake laye
COVER with top cake layer.
SPREAD remaining pudding mixture over top and sides of cake.
SPRINKLE one heart with icing sugar and the other heart with cocoa.
DECORATE sides of cake attractively with toasted almonds.
PIPE reserved whipped cream around edge of cake.

Recipe No. 440	Hungary

Hunyadi Torte

Batter:

8	egg yolks	8	
250 g	sugar	1¼	cups
1 pkg	**oetker** vanilla sugar	1	pkg.
8	egg whites	8	
200 g	ground hazelnuts	2	cups
100 g	semi-sweet chocolate, grated	4	sq.

Filling:

500 mL	whipping cream	2	cups
15 mL	sugar	1	tbsp.
2 pkgs	**oetker** Whip-it	2	pkgs.
5 drops	**oetker** rum flavouring concentrate	5	drops

Glaze:

1 pkg	**oetker** Chocofix	1	pkg.
	OR		
175 g	semi-sweet chocolate, chopped	7	sq.
100 g	sweet (unsalted) butter	½	cup

Decoration:

100 g	chopped hazelnuts	1	cup
	whole hazelnuts		

Batter:
PREHEAT oven to 190°C (375°F). Grease a 24 cm (9½″) springform pan.
CREAM egg yolks, sugar and vanilla sugar together on high speed of electric mixer until light and fluffy.
BEAT egg whites to stiff peaks.
FOLD egg whites, ground hazelnuts and chocolate into creamed mixture, gently but thoroughly.
TURN about 375 mL (1½ cups) batter into prepared pan.
BAKE on middle oven rack at 190°C (375°F) for 15-20 minutes.
REMOVE from pan.
REPEAT last three steps 3 times to obtain 4 layers.
Filling:
BEAT whipping cream in mixer bowl to soft peaks. Gradually add sugar, Whip-it and flavouring concentrate, beating to stiff peaks.
SPREAD filling evenly over cooled cake layers.
PUT cake layers together.
Glaze:
SOFTEN Chocofix as directed on package OR
COMBINE chocolate and butter in top of double boiler. Place over simmering water, stirring constantly until melted.
SPREAD over top and sides of torte. Before hardening completely, sprinkle sides with chopped hazelnuts.
DECORATE top with whole hazelnuts.

Recipe No. 441	England

Apple Pie

Dough:

250 g	all-purpose flour	1⅔	cups
80 g	shortening	½	cup
130 g	butter or margarine, softened	⅔	cup
pinch	salt		pinch
90-120 mL	cold water	6-8	tbsp.

Filling:

1 kg	apples	2	lbs.
80 g	sugar	⅓	cup
1 btl	**oetker** lemon flavouring concentrate	1	btl.
10 mL	cinnamon	2	tsp.
pinch	ginger		pinch
pinch	allspice		pinch
pinch	nutmeg		pinch

Glaze:

1	egg yolk, slightly beaten	1	
30 mL	water	2	tbsp.

Batter:
PREHEAT oven to 200°C (400°F). Grease a 25 cm (10″) springform pan.
SIFT flour onto pastry board. Make a well in centre.
PUT shortening, butter, salt and water in well.
WORK all ingredients together quickly to make a smooth dough. Chill slightly for easy rolling, about 30 minutes.
DIVIDE dough into 3 equal portions.
PRESS or roll ⅓ of dough onto prepared pan.
SHAPE ⅓ of dough into a long roll. Press around inside rim of pan forming 4 cm (1½″) sides. Press seams to seal.
Filling:
PEEL and core apples. Cut into thin slices.
MIX with sugar, flavouring concentrate and spices.
SPREAD filling evenly over dough.
ROLL out remaining dough.
PLACE dough over filling. Press sides together to seal.
DECORATE with pastry scraps as illustrated.
COMBINE egg yolk and water.
BRUSH egg mixture over dough.
BAKE on middle oven rack at 200°C (400°F) for 45-55 minutes.

Sicilian Torte

Batter:

Metric	Ingredient	Imperial
5	egg yolks	5
250 g	sugar	1 cup
1 pkg	**oetker** vanilla sugar	1 pkg.
5	egg whites	5
250 g	all-purpose flour	1⅔ cups
pinch	**oetker** baking powder	pinch
Filling:		
500 g	Mascarpone cheese, Quark or soft cream cheese	1 lb.
50 g	icing sugar, sifted	⅓ cup
60 g	chopped almonds	½ cup
50 g	semi-sweet chocolate, grated	2 sq.
100 g	mixed candied fruit, chopped	¾ cup
75 mL	Marsala (sweet red wine)	⅓ cup
Glaze:		
250 g	icing sugar, sifted	1¾ cups
30-45 mL	lemon juice	2-3 tbsp.
Decoration:		
	sliced almonds	
	chopped candied fruit	

Batter:
PREHEAT oven to 180°C (350°F). Grease a 24 cm (9½″) springform pan.
CREAM egg yolks, ⅔ of sugar and vanilla sugar together on high speed of electric mixer until fluffy.
BEAT egg whites and remaining sugar to stiff peaks.
FOLD egg whites into creamed mixture gently.
SIFT flour and baking powder together over creame mixture. Fold in gently but thoroughly.
TURN batter into prepared pan.
BAKE on middle oven rack at 180°C (350°F) for 35-40 minutes.
REMOVE from pan immediately. Let cool completel
SLICE cake horizontally to make 2 layers.

Filling:
CREAM Mascarpone cheese and icing sugar togethe on high speed of electric mixer until smooth.
COMBINE almonds, grated chocolate, fruit and Marsala. Add to cheese mixture. Mix well.
SPREAD filling evenly over bottom cake layer.
COVER with top cake layer. Chill 30 minutes.

Glaze:
COMBINE icing sugar and lemon juice to make a thick glaze consistency. Pour over cake.
DECORATE sides of cake with almond slices and tc of cake with candied fruit.

Swedish Mazarin Torte

Dough:

Metric	Ingredient	Imperial
150 g	butter or margarine, softened	⅔ cup
40 g	sugar	¼ cup
1 pkg	**oetker** natural vanilla sugar	1 pkg.
pinch	salt	pinch
2	egg yolks	2
200 g	all-purpose flour	1⅓ cups
Filling:		
120 g	butter or margarine, softened	½ cup
100 g	icing sugar, sifted	⅔ cup
2	eggs	2
½ btl	**oetker** rum flavouring concentrate	½ btl.
½ btl	**oetker** lemon flavouring concentrate	½ btl.
150 g	ground almonds	1½ cups
20 g	all-purpose flour	2 tbsp.
Decoration:		
	blanched whole almonds toasted, syrup	

Dough:
PREHEAT oven to 180°C (350°F). Grease a 25 cm (10″) fluted or plain springform pan or flan pan.
CREAM butter in mixer bowl. Gradually add sugar, vanilla sugar, salt and egg yolks.
BEAT at medium speed until light and fluffy.
SIFT flour over egg mixture. Fold in gently but thoroughly. Chill 2 hours for easy rolling.
PRESS or roll ⅔ of dough onto base of prepared par
SHAPE remaining dough into a long roll. Press arou inside rim of pan forming 3 cm (1¼″) sides. Press seams to seal.
BAKE on middle oven rack at 180°C (350°F) for 10 minutes.

Filling:
CREAM butter in mixer bowl. Gradually add icing sugar, eggs and flavouring concentrates, beating until light and fluffy. Stir in ground almonds and flour.
SPREAD filling evenly over dough.
BAKE on middle oven rack at 180°C (350°F) for 30-40 minutes.
DECORATE cake with toasted almonds and syrup.

Regal Torte

Batter:

7	egg yolks	7	
150 g	sugar	¾	cup
1 pkg	**oetker** vanilla sugar	1	pkg.
7	egg whites	7	
150 g	all-purpose flour	1	cup

Creme:

1 pkg	**oetker** vanilla pudding powder	1	pkg.
100 g	sugar	½	cup
500 mL	milk	2	cups
250 g	butter or margarine, softened	1¼	cups
50 g	cocoa, sifted	½	cup
100 g	semi-sweet chocolate, melted	4	sq.

Glaze:

1 pkg	**oetker** Chocofix OR	1	pkg.
175 g	semi-sweet chocolate, chopped	7	sq.
100 g	sweet (unsalted) butter	½	cup

Decoration:

marzipan roses

Batter:
PREHEAT oven to 220°C (425°F). Grease a 25 cm (10") springform pan. Line with waxed paper. Grease again.
BEAT egg yolks, ½ of sugar and vanilla sugar together on high speed of electric mixer until light and fluffy.
BEAT egg whites and remaining sugar to stiff peaks.
FOLD egg whites gently into creamed mixture.
SIFT flour over egg mixture. Fold in gently but thoroughly.
TURN approx 250 mL (1 cup) batter into prepared pan.
BAKE on middle oven rack at 220°C (425°F) for 6-9 minutes.
REMOVE from pan.
REPEAT last three steps 5 times to obtain 6 layers.
Creme:
PREPARE pudding according to package directions.
COOL to room temperature, stirring occasionally.
CREAM butter. Beat in pudding 1 spoonful at a time alternately with sifted cocoa and melted chocolate. (Butter and pudding must be at the same temperature to prevent curdling.)
PUT aside some creme for sides and top of cake.
SPREAD remaining filling dividing evenly over cooled cake layers.
PUT cake layers together.
SPREAD creme over top and sides of cake.
REFRIGERATE for 1 hour.
Glaze:
SOFTEN Chocofix as directed on package OR
COMBINE chocolate and butter in top of double boiler. Place over simmering water, stirring constantly until melted.
SPREAD over top and sides of torte.
DECORATE with marzipan roses.

INTERNATIONAL

CAKE RECIPES

Recipe No. 445 Switzerlan

Summer Cake

Dough:

500 g	all-purpose flour	3⅓ cups	
1 pkg	**oetker** instant dry yeast	1 pkg.	
120 g	sugar	1¼ cups	
1 pkg	**oetker** vanilla sugar	1 pkg.	
pinch	salt	pinch	
1	egg	1	
120 g	butter or margarine, melted	1¼ cups	
approx 250 mL	lukewarm milk	1 cup	

Filling:

200 g	ground almonds	2 cups
200 g	sugar	1 cup
3 drops	**oetker** almond flavouring concentrate	3 drops
pinch	cinnamon	pinch
40 g	butter or margarine, softened	¼ cup
2	eggs	2

Glaze:

1	egg, slightly beaten	1

Decoration:

25 g	sugar sprinkles	2 tbsp.

Dough:
PREHEAT oven to 200°C (400°F). Grease a 26 cm (10½″) springform pan.
COMBINE flour and yeast in large bowl. Make a wel in centre.
PUT sugar, vanilla sugar, salt, egg and melted butter in well.
WORK flour into centre ingredients, gradually adding milk.
KNEAD dough with dough hooks or by hand until blistered and shiny in appearance and no longer stick about 5 minutes.
LET RISE, covered, in warm place until doubled in size, about 1 hour.
KNEAD again. Roll out ½ of dough.
PRESS onto bottom and sides of prepared springforn pan.
Filling:
COMBINE almonds, sugar, flavouring concentrate an cinnamon. Mix well.
CREAM butter and eggs together thoroughly. Gradually add almond mixture. Mix well.
SPREAD filling evenly over dough.
ROLL out remaining dough into a 26 cm (10½″) diameter round.
CUT with sharp knife from centre, leaving rim intact, forming 18 strands.
SHAPE into braids; see photo.
PLACE braided top layer over filling. Press sides together to seal. Brush with beaten egg.
DECORATE with sugar sprinkles.
BAKE on middle oven rack at 200°C (400°F) for 35-40 minutes.

Recipe No. 446 Russi

Russian Hazelnut Cake

Batter:

170 g	butter or margarine, softened	⅔ cup
200 g	sugar	1 cup
4	eggs	4
60 mL	whipping cream	¼ cup
30 g	liquid honey	2 tbsp.
80 g	all-purpose flour	½ cup
5 mL	**oetker** baking powder	1 tsp.
130 g	ground hazelnuts	1⅓ cups

Decoration:

100 g	liquid honey	⅓ cup
130 g	icing sugar, sifted	1 cup
15 mL	water	1 tbsp.
15 mL	lemon juice	1 tbsp.
50 g	whole hazelnuts	½ cup

Batter:
PREHEAT oven to 180°C (350°F). Grease and flour loaf pan.
CREAM butter in mixer bowl. Gradually add sugar, eggs, whipping cream and honey.
BEAT at medium speed until light and fluffy.
COMBINE flour and baking powder. Add to creamec mixture. Stir in hazelnuts. Mix well.
TURN batter into prepared pan.
BAKE on middle oven rack at 180°C (350°F) for 40-45 minutes.
REMOVE cake from pan.
SPREAD liquid honey over top and sides of cake.
LET cool completely.
COMBINE icing sugar, water and lemon juice to mal a thick glaze consistency. Pour over cake.
DECORATE with hazelnuts.

Alsatian Apple Cake

Dough:

200	g	all-purpose flour	1⅓ cups
½	pkg	**oetker** baking powder (7 g/2 tsp.)	½ pkg.
80	g	sugar	⅓ cup
1		egg	1
	pinch	salt	pinch
100	g	butter or margarine, cold	½ cup

Filling:

1000	g	apples, peeled and cored	2 lbs.

Glaze:

2		eggs	2
100	g	sugar	½ cup
2	pkg	**oetker** vanilla sugar	2 pkg.
75	mL	whipping cream	⅓ cup
75	mL	cold milk	⅓ cup

Dough:
PREHEAT oven to 180°C (350°F). Grease a 26 cm (10½″) fluted or plain springform pan.
SIFT flour and baking powder onto pastry board. Make a well in centre.
PUT sugar, egg and salt in well. Work a little flour into centre mixture.
CUT cold butter into small pieces over flour mixture
WORK all ingredients together quickly to make a smooth dough.
CHILL slightly for easy rolling, about 30 minutes.
PRESS or roll dough onto bottom and sides of prepared pan.
Filling:
PEEL and core apples. Cut into thin slices.
PLACE attractively over dough.
BAKE on middle oven rack at 180°C (350°F) for 20 minutes.
Glaze:
COMBINE eggs, sugar, vanilla sugar, whipping crea and milk. Mix well.
POUR evenly over cake.
BAKE on middle oven rack at 180°C (350°F) for 20 minutes longer.
REMOVE rim from pan immediately. Let cool.

Apple Strudel

Pastry:

1	pkg	frozen puff pastry (397 g/14 oz.)	1 pkg.

Filling:

500	g	apples	1 lb.
50	g	butter or margarine	¼ cup
60	mL	Calvados	¼ cup
50	g	sugar	¼ cup
½	btl	**oetker** lemon flavouring concentrate	½ btl.
3	mL	ground cinnamon	¾ tsp.
40	g	raisins	⅓ cup
25	g	ground hazelnuts	¼ cup
1		egg yolk, slightly beaten	1

Decoration:

100	g	icing sugar, sifted	⅔ cup
15-30	mL	water or lemon juice	1-2 tbsp.

Pastry:
PREHEAT oven to 220°C (425°F). Rinse baking sh with cold water.
THAW puff pastry according to package directions.
ROLL out pastry into rectangle about 5 mm (¼″) thickness.
Filling:
PEEL, core and grate apples.
HEAT butter in saucepan.
ADD apples. Cook gently for 3 minutes.
POUR Calvados over apples.
ADD sugar, flavouring concentrate, cinnamon, raisir and hazelnuts.
LET cool.
SPREAD apple mixture evenly over ½ of pastry.
ROLL up tightly starting at end with filling.
BRUSH lightly with beaten egg yolk.
PLACE onto prepared baking sheet.
BAKE on middle oven rack at 220°C (425°F) for 30-45 minutes.
COMBINE icing sugar and water or lemon juice to make a thin glaze consistency. Spread over strudel.
CUT strudel into serving pieces with sharp knife.
SERVE warm or cool.

Recipe No. 449 — England

Spice Cake

Batter:

230 g	butter or margarine, softened	1	cup
230 g	brown sugar	1	cup
1 pkg	**oetker** natural vanilla sugar	1	pkg.
4	eggs	4	
50 g	ground almonds	½	cup
230 g	all-purpose flour	1½	cups
10 mL	**oetker** baking powder	2	tsp.
5 mL	ground cloves	1	tsp.
3 mL	ground cinnamon	¾	tsp.
2 mL	baking soda	¼	tsp.

Glaze:

80 mL	evaporated milk	⅓	cup
40 g	butter or margarine	2	tbsp.
180 g	sugar	¾	cup
1 pkg	**oetker** vanilla sugar	1	pkg.

Decoration:

walnut halves

Batter:
PREHEAT oven to 180°C (350°F). Grease a 24 cm (9½") springform pan or fluted bundt cake pan.
CREAM butter in mixer bowl. Gradually add brown sugar, vanilla sugar, eggs and ground almonds. Mix well.
COMBINE flour, baking powder, spices and baking soda. Add to creamed mixture. Mix well.
TURN batter into prepared pan.
BAKE on middle oven rack at 180°C (350°F) for 55-65 minutes.
Glaze:
COMBINE evaporated milk, butter and sugar in sma saucepan. Cook on low heat for 30 minutes, stirring occasionally.
REMOVE from heat. Stir in vanilla sugar.
BEAT with electric mixer at medium speed until mixture starts to thicken.
POUR over cake. Spread quickly with a wet knife.
DECORATE with walnuts.

Recipe No. 450 — Yugoslav

Regal Cheese Slices

Dough:

400 g	all-purpose flour	2⅔	cups
10 mL	**oetker** baking powder	2	tsp.
100 g	icing sugar, sifted	⅔	cup
1 pkg	**oetker** vanilla sugar	1	pkg.
1	egg yolk	1	
200 g	butter or margarine, cold	1	cup

Filling:

4	egg yolks	4	
30 mL	hot water	2	tbsp.
100 g	sugar	½	cup
1 pkg	**oetker** vanilla sugar	1	pkg.
5 drops	**oetker** lemon flavouring concentrate	5	drops
500 g	cottage cheese (20% fat)	1	lb.
250 mL	whipping cream	1	cup
5	egg whites	5	

Glaze:

1	egg yolk, slightly beaten	1	

Dough:
PREHEAT oven to 180°C (350°F). Grease a baking sheet.
SIFT flour and baking powder onto pastry board. Make a well in centre.
PUT icing sugar, vanilla sugar and egg yolk in well. Work a little flour into centre mixture.
CUT cold butter into small pieces over flour mixture
WORK all ingredients together quickly to make a smooth dough.
CHILL slightly for easy rolling, about 30 minutes.
ROLL out dough to 5 mm (¼") thickness.
DIVIDE into two portions.
PLACE one portion onto prepared baking sheet.
Filling:
COMBINE egg yolks, water, ⅔ of sugar, vanilla suga and flavouring concentrate in mixer bowl.
BEAT with electric mixer at high speed until fluffy.
GRADUALLY add cottage cheese and whipping cream.
BEAT egg whites to soft peaks. Gradually add remaining sugar beating to stiff peaks.
FOLD into egg yolk mixture, gently but thoroughly.
SPREAD filling evenly onto bottom pastry layer.
COVER with top pastry layer.
BRUSH lightly with beaten egg yolk.
BAKE on middle oven rack at 180°C (350°F) for 40-50 minutes.
CUT into serving pieces. Serve warm or cool.

Recipe No. 451 — Czechoslovak

Moravian Apricot Cake

Batter:

50 g	butter or margarine, softened	¼ cup
120 g	sugar	½ cup
1 pkg	**oetker** vanilla sugar	1 pkg.
5	egg yolks	5
½ btl	**oetker** lemon flavouring concentrate	½ btl.
5	egg whites	5
80 g	all-purpose flour	½ cup
50 g	dry breadcrumbs	½ cup
10 mL	**oetker** baking powder	2 tsp.

Filling:

500 g	canned or steamed apricot halves	1 lb.

Decoration:

icing sugar

Batter:
PREHEAT oven to 190°C (375°F). Grease a fluted plain 24 cm (9½″) springform pan.
COMBINE butter, ½ of sugar, vanilla sugar, egg yol and flavouring concentrate in mixer bowl. Beat at h speed of electric mixer until light and fluffy.
BEAT egg whites to soft peaks. Gradually add remaining sugar, beating to stiff peaks.
FOLD into egg yolk mixture.
COMBINE flour, breadcrumbs and baking powder. Mix well. Fold into egg mixture, gently but thoroug
TURN batter into prepared pan.
BAKE on middle oven rack at 190°C (375°F) for 20 minutes.
Filling:
PLACE apricot halves, round side up, on partially baked cake.
BAKE for 10-15 minutes longer.
COOL cake in pan for 10 minutes, then remove and let cool completely.
SPRINKLE with icing sugar.

Recipe No. 452 — Rus

Petersburg Rum Baba

Dough:

400 g	all-purpose flour	2⅔ cups
1 pkg	**oetker** instant dry yeast	1 pkg.
100 g	icing sugar, sifted	⅔ cup
pinch	salt	pinch
5 drops	**oetker** rum flavouring concentrate	5 drops
3	eggs	3
100 g	butter or margarine, melted	½ cup
125 mL	lukewarm milk	½ cup

Syrup:

250 g	frozen strawberries	8 oz.
125 mL	warm water	½ cup
125 mL	rum	½ cup
50 g	sugar	¼ cup
1 pkg	**oetker** vanilla sugar	1 pkg.

Decoration:

strawberries

Method:
PREHEAT oven to 160°C (325°F). Grease small ba or ring pans.
COMBINE flour and yeast in large mixing bowl. M a well in centre.
PUT icing sugar, salt, flavouring concentrate, eggs a melted butter in well.
WORK flour into centre ingredients, gradually addi milk.
KNEAD dough with dough hooks or by hand until blistered and shiny in appearance and no longer sti about 5 minutes.
LET stand covered, in warm place, about 30 minute
KNEAD again.
PLACE dough in prepared pans, filling half full.
LET RISE, covered, until doubled in size.
BAKE on middle oven rack at 160°C (325°F) for 40-45 minutes.
REMOVE from pans immediately.
Syrup:
COMBINE frozen strawberries, water, sugar, rum a vanilla sugar.
LET stand for 30 minutes.
POUR liquid from strawberry mixture into cleaned baba pans.
REPLACE cakes in pans. Let soak up all liquid.
REMOVE from pans.
DECORATE with strawberries.

Recipe No. 453 Englar

Rum Raisin Cake

Batter:

250 g	raisins	2½ cups
30 g	chopped candied orange peel	⅓ cup
30 g	candied cherries, chopped	⅓ cup
30 g	chopped walnuts	¼ cup
45 mL	rum	3 tbsp.
pinch	cinnamon	pinch
pinch	nutmeg	pinch
pinch	ground cloves	pinch
50 g	butter or margarine, softened	¼ cup
80 g	icing sugar, sifted	½ cup
1 pkg	**oetker** vanilla sugar	1 pkg.
15 mL	liquid honey	1 tbsp.
2	eggs	2
100 g	all-purpose flour	⅔ cup
5 mL	**oetker** baking powder	1 tsp.

Decoration:

chopped mixed candied fruit

Batter:
PREHEAT oven to 180°C (350°F). Grease and flour fluted pan or 1.5 L (8½″ × 4½″) loaf pan.
COMBINE fruits, walnuts, rum and spices. Let stanc for 30 minutes. Mix well.
CREAM butter, icing sugar, vanilla sugar, honey and eggs together in mixer bowl.
SIFT flour and baking powder over creamed mixture
ADD fruit mixture.
FOLD in gently but thoroughly.
TURN batter into prepared pan.
BAKE on middle oven rack at 180°C (350°F) for 60 minutes.
REMOVE from pan immediately. Decorate with candied fruit.

Recipe No. 454 Spa

Andalusian Cake

125 mL	water	½ cup
125 mL	cherry brandy	½ cup
30 g	sugar	¼ cup
200 g	lady fingers	24

Filling:

250 g	semi-sweet chocolate	10 sq.
2	egg yolks, slightly beaten	2
60 mL	water	¼ cup

Decoration:

375 mL	whipping cream	1½ cups
1 pkg	**oetker** Whip-it	1 pkg.
1 pkg	**oetker** vanilla sugar	1 pkg.

Method:
COVER bottom of loaf pan with foil paper.
COMBINE water, cherry brandy and sugar in small saucepan. Bring to a boil. Let cool.
DIP lady fingers in cherry mixture. Let soak.
ARRANGE ⅓ of lady fingers in bottom of loaf pan.
Filling:
MELT chocolate in top of double boiler.
ADD beaten egg yolks and water. Mix well.
POUR ½ of mixture over lady fingers in loaf pan.
ARRANGE ½ of remaining lady fingers over chocolate mixture.
POUR remaining chocolate mixture over lady fingers
ARRANGE remaining lady fingers over chocolate mixture.
COVER with foil paper.
LET harden in freezer, 1-2 hours.
REMOVE from pan.
Decoration:
BEAT whipping cream to soft peaks. Gradually add Whip-it and vanilla sugar, beating to stiff peaks.
DECORATE cake attractively.
REFRIGERATE until serving time.

Recipe No. 455 Rus

Russian Easter Bread

Dough:

500 g	all-purpose flour	3⅓	cups
1 pkg	**oetker** instant dry yeast	1	pkg.
100 g	sugar	½	cup
pinch	salt		pinch
¼ btl	**oetker** lemon flavouring concentrate	¼	btl.
¼ btl	**oetker** rum flavouring concentrate	¼	btl.
3	eggs	3	
100 g	butter or margarine, melted	½	cup
125 mL	lukewarm milk	½	cup
100 g	raisins	1	cup
50 g	chopped candied orange	½	cup
50 g	chopped almonds	½	cup
50 g	butter or margarine, melted	¼	cup

Dough:
PREHEAT oven to 180°C (350°F). Grease a bakin sheet.
COMBINE flour and yeast in mixing bowl. Make a well in centre. Put sugar, salt, flavouring concentrat eggs and melted butter in well. Work flour into cen ingredients, gradually adding milk.
KNEAD dough with dough hooks or by hand until blistered and shiny in appearance and no longer sti about 5 minutes.
LET RISE, covered, in warm place, about 40 minu
COMBINE fruit and almonds. Mix into dough. Kn well. Shape into a round loaf. Place onto prepared baking sheet.
LET RISE, covered, in warm place, about 30 minu
CUT diamond pattern on top of loaf with sharp kn
BAKE on middle oven rack at 180°C (350°F) for 35-45 minutes. Brush with melted butter while warr

Recipe No. 456 Czechoslova

Egerlander Poppy Seed Crumb Cake

Dough:

300 g	all-purpose flour	2	cups
1 pkg	**oetker** instant dry yeast	1	pkg.
60 g	sugar	⅓	cup
pinch	salt		pinch
1	egg	1	
100 g	butter or margarine, melted	½	cup
125 mL	lukewarm milk	½	cup

Poppy seed filling:

500 mL	milk	2	cups
5 drops	**oetker** lemon flavouring	5	drops
100 g	cream of wheat	½	cup
300 g	ground poppy seeds	2	cups
150 g	sugar	¾	cup
40 mL	liquid honey	2	tbsp.
100 g	raisins	1	cup
5 mL	ground cinnamon	1	tsp.

Cottage cheese filling:

2	egg yolks	2	
80 g	sugar	½	cup
1 pkg	**oetker** vanilla sugar	1	pkg.
250 g	cottage cheese	1¼	cups

Plum filling:

250 g	plums, cooked, pitted	½	lb.
15 mL	rum	1	tbsp.

Crumb Topping:

100 g	all-purpose flour	⅔	cup
50 g	sugar	¼	cup
50 g	butter or margarine, cold	¼	cup

Dough:
PREHEAT oven to 200°C (400°F). Grease a baking sl
COMBINE flour and yeast in large bowl. Make a v in centre, add sugar, salt, egg and melted butter.
WORK flour into centre ingredients, gradually add milk.
KNEAD dough with dough hooks or by hand until blistered and shiny in appearance and no longer sti about 5 minutes.
LET RISE, covered, in warm place until doubled in size, about 1 hour. Knead again.
ROLL out dough to 5 mm (¼″) thickness.
PLACE onto baking sheet.

Poppy seed filling:
COMBINE milk and flavouring concentrate in saucepan. Bring to boil. Stir in cream of wheat. Co
STIR poppy seeds, sugar, honey, raisins and cinnar into mixture. Mix well.

Cheese filling:
CREAM egg yolks, sugar and vanilla sugar togethe mixing bowl. Add cottage cheese, mixing until smo

Plum filling:
COMBINE plums and rum. Mix well.

Crumb topping:
COMBINE flour and sugar.
CUT cold butter into small pieces over mixture.
WORK dough with fork to form crumbs.
SPREAD poppy seed filling evenly over rolled out do
SPREAD cheese filling and plum filling alternately over poppy seed filling.
SPRINKLE crumbs evenly over filling.
BAKE on middle oven rack at 200°C (400°F) for 30-35 minutes.

Recipe No. 457 I t

Panettone

Batter:

8	egg yolks	8	
160 g	sugar	¾	cup
50 g	chopped dates	½	cup
50 g	chopped figs	½	cup
50 g	chopped almonds	½	cup
50 g	chopped candied orange peel	½	cup
50 g	chopped candied lemon peel	½	cup
50 g	raisins	½	cup
100 g	semi-sweet chocolate, grated	4	sq.
8	egg whites	8	
150 g	all-purpose flour	1	cup

Glaze:

100 g	icing sugar, sifted	⅔	cup
15-30 mL	lemon juice	1-2	tbsp.

Decoration:

whole dates, sliced

Batter:
PREHEAT oven to 190°C (375°F). Grease and flo
24 cm (9½″) springform pan.
CREAM egg yolks and sugar together with electric mixer until thick.
ADD fruit, chocolate and almonds to egg yolk mixture. Mix well.
BEAT egg whites to stiff peaks.
FOLD into fruit mixture.
SIFT flour over fruit mixture. Fold in gently but thoroughly.
TURN batter into prepared pan.
BAKE on middle oven rack at 190°C (375°F) for 50-60 minutes.
REMOVE from pan. Let cool.

Glaze:
COMBINE icing sugar and lemon juice to make a thick glaze consistency. Pour over cake.
DECORATE with slices of date.

Recipe No. 458 I t

Red Currant Slices

Dough:

150 g	all-purpose flour	1	cup
250 g	ground almonds	2½	cups
150 g	sugar	¾	cup
1 pkg	**oetker** vanilla sugar	1	pkg.
pinch	ground cinnamon		pinch
5 drops	**oetker** lemon flavouring concentrate	5	drops
2	eggs	2	
200 g	butter or margarine, cold	1	cup

Filling:

100 g	red currant jam or marmalade	½	cup
1	egg white, slightly beaten	1	

Glaze:

30 mL	hot water	2	tbsp.
30 mL	lemon juice	2	tbsp.
120 g	icing sugar, sifted	½	cup

Dough:
PREHEAT oven to 190°C (375°F). Grease a bakir sheet.
SIFT flour onto pastry board.
MIX with ground almonds. Make a well in centre.
PUT sugar, vanilla sugar, cinnamon, flavouring concentrate and eggs in well.
WORK a little flour into mixture.
CUT cold butter into small pieces over flour mixtu
WORK all ingredients together quickly to make a smooth dough.
CHILL slightly for easy rolling, about 1 hour.
ROLL out dough to 5 mm (¼″) thickness.
DIVIDE into two equal portions.
PLACE one portion onto prepared baking sheet.
SPREAD evenly with jam. Leave 1 cm (⅓″) rim fr
BRUSH rim with beaten egg white.
COVER with top layer. Press rims together firmly to seal.
BAKE on middle oven rack at 190°C (375°F) for 30-40 minutes.

Glaze:
COMBINE water, lemon juice and icing sugar to r a thick glaze consistency.
POUR evenly over warm pastry.
CUT into serving pieces.

Recipe No. 459 Ita

Heavenly Delight

Batter:

4	egg yolks	4	
160 g	sugar	¾	cup
1 pkg	**oetker** vanilla sugar	1	pkg.
4	egg whites	4	
160 g	all-purpose flour	1	cup
pinch	**oetker** baking powder		pinch

Syrup:

45 mL	rum	3	tbsp.
45 mL	cognac	3	tbsp.
30 mL	cherry brandy	2	tbsp.

Filling:

500 mL	whipping cream	2	cups
100 g	icing sugar, sifted	⅔	cup
40 g	ground almonds, toasted and cooled	½	cup
40 g	ground hazelnuts, toasted and cooled	½	cup
100 g	semi-sweet chocolate, grated	4	sq.
3 drops	**oetker** almond flavouring concentrate	3	drops

Decoration:

icing sugar, sifted
cocoa, sifted

Batter:
PREHEAT oven to 190°C (375°F). Grease a jelly rol
pan. Line with waxed paper. Grease again.
BEAT egg yolks, ½ of sugar and vanilla sugar on hig
speed of electric mixer until thick and creamy.
BEAT egg whites to soft peaks. Gradually add remaining sugar, beating to stiff peaks.
FOLD into egg yolk mixture.
SIFT flour and baking powder over mixture. Fold in gently but thoroughly.
SPREAD batter onto prepared pan 1 cm (⅓″) high.
BAKE on middle oven rack at 190°C (375°F) for 10-12 minutes.
SPRINKLE waxed paper or tea towel with sugar.
REMOVE cake immediately onto prepared waxed paper or tea towel. Take off waxed paper carefully from cake. Let cool.
POUR rum, cognac and cherry brandy evenly over cake.
LINE a bowl (18 cm/7″ diameter) with plastic wrap.
COVER bottom and sides of prepared bowl with ⅔ cake.

Filling:
BEAT whipping cream to soft peaks. Gradually add icing sugar. Beat to stiff peaks.
FOLD toasted almonds and hazelnuts, grated chocolate and flavouring concentrate into cream.
POUR nut mixture evenly onto cake.
COVER with remaining cake.
REFRIGERATE for 2-4 hours.
TURN bowl over onto serving plate. Remove plastic wrap.
SPRINKLE with icing sugar and cocoa.

Recipe No. 460 Ameri

Banana Nut Cake

Batter:

20 g	vegetable oil	2	tbsp.
350 g	mashed bananas	1½	cups
200 g	sugar	1	cup
45 mL	milk	3	tbsp.
2	eggs	2	
250 g	all-purpose flour	1⅔	cups
3 mL	**oetker** baking powder	¾	tsp.
3 mL	baking soda	¾	tsp.
pinch	salt		pinch
100 g	chopped hazelnuts	1	cup

Decoration:

2	bananas	2	
	juice of ½ lemon		

Batter:
PREHEAT oven to 180°C (350°F). Grease a 24 cm (9½″) springform pan.
COMBINE oil, mashed bananas and sugar together i mixer bowl. Beat at medium speed. Gradually add milk and eggs.
COMBINE flour, baking powder, baking soda and salt. Add to banana mixture. Mix well.
STIR in hazelnuts. Mix well.
TURN batter into prepared pan.
SLICE bananas.
SPRINKLE with lemon juice.
DISTRIBUTE evenly on cake.
BAKE on middle oven rack at 180°C (350°F) for 60-70 minutes.

Recipe No. 461 Denm

Iceland Roll

Batter:

5	egg yolks	5	
100 g	sugar	½	cup
1 pkg	**oetker** vanilla sugar	1	pkg.
5	egg whites	5	
120 g	all-purpose flour	¾	cup
pinch	**oetker** baking powder		pinch

Filling:

500 mL	vanilla ice cream	2	cups
500 mL	strawberry ice cream	2	cups
	candied cherries		

Glaze:

1 pkg	**oetker** Chocofix OR	1	pkg.
200 g	semi-sweet chocolate, chopped	8	sq.
120 g	sweet (unsalted) butter	½	cup

Decoration:

100 g	icing sugar, sifted	⅔	cup
15-30 mL	lemon juice	1-2	tbsp.

Batter:
PREHEAT oven to 180°C (350°F). Grease a jelly r
pan. Line with waxed paper. Grease again.
BEAT egg yolks, ⅔ of sugar and vanilla sugar on hi
speed of electric mixer until thick and creamy.
BEAT egg whites to soft peaks. Gradually add remaining sugar, beating to stiff peaks.
FOLD into egg yolk mixture.
SIFT flour and baking powder over egg mixture. Fo
in gently but thoroughly.
SPREAD batter onto prepared pan 1 cm (⅓") high
BAKE on middle oven rack at 180°C (350°F) for 10-12 minutes.
SPRINKLE waxed paper or a tea towel with sugar.
REMOVE cake immediately onto prepared waxed paper or tea towel. Take off waxed paper carefully from cake. Let cool.
LINE a loaf pan with foil paper.
COVER bottom and sides of pan with ⅔ of cake.
Filling:
SLICE ice cream.
PLACE strawberry ice cream onto cake.
COVER with layer of candied cherries.
PLACE vanilla ice cream over cherries.
COVER with remaining cake layer, pressing firmly around ice cream.
LET FREEZE for 3-4 hours, or until firm.
DIP pan quickly into hot water and remove cake to
serving plate. Remove foil.
Glaze:
SOFTEN Chocofix as directed on package OR
MELT chocolate and butter together, stirring until smooth.
POUR evenly over cake.
COMBINE icing sugar and lemon juice to make a thick glaze consistency.
DECORATE cake attractively.

Recipe No. 462 It

Coffee Squares

30-40	lady fingers	30-40	
250 mL	cold strong coffee	1	cup

Filling:

4	egg yolks	4	
100 g	sugar	½	cup
1 pkg	**oetker** vanilla sugar	1	pkg.
500 g	Mascarpone, Quark or soft cream cheese	1	lb.
60 mL	egg liqueur	¼	cup
4	egg whites	4	

Decoration:

cocoa

Method:
DIP lady fingers in cold coffee. Let soak.
COMBINE egg yolks, sugar and vanilla sugar in m
bowl.
BEAT at high speed of electric mixer until thick ar
light. Gradually add Mascarpone and egg liqueur, beating until smooth.
BEAT egg whites to stiff peaks.
FOLD into egg yolk mixture, gently but thoroughl
PLACE ½ of lady fingers in shallow bowl.
SPREAD ½ of filling over lady fingers.
COVER with remaining lady fingers and remainin
filling.
SIFT cocoa lightly over filling.
REFRIGERATE for 3-4 hours. Refrigerate left-ov

Recipe No. 463 France

Parisian Chocolate Roll

Batter:

4	egg yolks	4
60 mL	hot water	¼ cup
200 g	sugar	1 cup
1 pkg	**oetker** vanilla sugar	1 pkg.
4	egg whites	4
60 g	all-purpose flour	⅓ cup
60 g	**oetker** cornstarch	⅓ cup
40 g	cocoa	½ cup
½ pkg	**oetker** baking powder (7 g/2 tsp)	½ pkg.

Filling:

250 mL	whipping cream	1 cup
250 g	semi-sweet chocolate, chopped	10 sq.

Glaze:

1 pkg	**oetker** Chocofix OR	1 pkg
150 g	semi-sweet chocolate, chopped	6 sq.
100 g	butter or margarine	½ cup

Decoration:

125 mL	whipping cream	½ cup

Batter:
PREHEAT oven to 200°C (400°F). Grease a jelly roll pan. Line with waxed paper. Grease again.
BEAT egg yolks and water together at high speed of electric mixer until light and fluffy. Gradually add ½ of sugar and vanilla sugar, beating until thick.
BEAT egg whites to stiff peaks. Gradually add remaining sugar, beating to stiff peaks.
FOLD carefully into egg yolk mixture.
COMBINE flour, cornstarch, cocoa and baking powder.
SIFT over egg yolk mixture. Gradually fold in gently but thoroughly.
SPREAD batter onto prepared pan. Bake on middle oven rack at 200°C (400°F) for 10-12 minutes.
SPRINKLE tea towel with sugar.
REMOVE cake immediately onto prepared tea towel. Take off waxed paper carefully from cake.
ROLL up warm cake carefully, leaving tea towel inside cake. Let cool.
Filling:
HEAT whipping cream and chocolate together. Bring to a boil, stirring constantly until melted.
POUR into a bowl. Let cool, stirring constantly. Refrigerate.
UNROLL cake carefully. Remove cloth.
SPREAD filling evenly over cake. Roll up carefully.
Glaze:
SOFTEN Chocofix as directed on package, OR HEAT chocolate and butter together, stirring until melted. Pour evenly over cake roll.
BEAT whipping cream to stiff peaks, decorate cake.

Recipe No. 464 Scotland

Dundee Cake

Batter:

130 g	butter or margarine, softened	¾ cup
30 g	marzipan	1 oz.
130 g	brown sugar	⅔ cup
3	eggs	3
15 mL	marmalade or apricot jam	1 tbsp.
180 g	all-purpose flour	1¼ cups
½ pkg	**oetker** baking powder (7 g/2 tsp)	½ pkg.
250 g	raisins	2½ cups
30 g	chopped candied orange peel	2 tbsp.
5 drops	**oetker** rum flavouring concentrate	5 drops

Decoration:

200 g	blanched whole almonds	7 oz.
	marmalade or apricot jam, strained	

Batter:
PREHEAT oven to 180°C (350°F). Grease and flour 24 cm (9½″) springform pan.
COMBINE butter, marzipan and brown sugar in mixing bowl. Beat at high speed of electric mixer until light and fluffy. Gradually add eggs and marmalade.
MIX very well, for about 10 minutes.
SIFT flour and baking powder together.
FOLD gradually into egg mixture.
SPRINKLE flavouring concentrate over fruit.
ADD carefully to batter. Turn into prepared pan.
DECORATE top evenly with almonds.
BAKE on middle oven rack at 180°C (350°F) for 60-70 minutes.
SPREAD marmalade evenly over almonds while cake is warm.

Recipe No. 465 Switzerl

Appenzell Nut Crescents

Dough:

500 g	all-purpose flour	3⅓ cups	
1 pkg	**oetker** instant dry yeast	1 pkg.	
80 g	sugar	½ cup	
1 pkg	**oetker** natural vanilla sugar	1 pkg.	
pinch	salt	pinch	
2	eggs	2	
80 g	butter or margarine, melted	½ cup	
approx 125 mL	lukewarm milk	½ cup	

Filling:

2	egg whites	2
60 g	sugar	⅓ cup
100 g	ground hazelnuts	1 cup

Glaze:

1	egg yolk, slightly beaten	1

Glaze:

30 g	butter or margarine, melted	2 tbsp.

Dough:
PREHEAT oven to 180°C (350°F). Grease a baki sheet.
COMBINE flour and yeast in large bowl. Make a in centre.
PUT sugar, vanilla sugar, salt, eggs and melted bu in well.
WORK flour into centre ingredients, gradually ad milk.
KNEAD dough with dough hooks or by hand un blistered and shiny in appearance and no longer s about 5 minutes.
PLACE in greased bowl.
LET RISE, covered in warm place until doubled size, about 1 hour.
KNEAD again.
ROLL out dough on floured surface to 5 mm (¼″ thickness.
CUT into squares 8 cm × 8 cm (3″ × 3″).
Filling:
BEAT egg whites and sugar to stiff peaks.
FOLD hazelnuts into egg white mixture, gently b thoroughly.
SPREAD nut mixture over dough. ROLL up fron point to opposite point.
PLACE onto prepared baking sheet.
BRUSH with beaten egg yolk.
BAKE on middle oven rack at 180°C (350°F) for 15-20 minutes.
BRUSH with melted butter while warm.

Recipe No. 466 Eng

Queen Elizabeth Cake

Batter:

125 g	chopped dates	1 cup
125 mL	boiling water	½ cup
60 g	butter or margarine, softened	⅓ cup
150 g	sugar	¾ cup
1 pkg	**oetker** natural vanilla sugar	1 pkg.
1	egg	1
40 g	chopped walnuts	⅓ cup
150 g	all-purpose flour	1 cup
5 mL	**oetker** baking powder	1 tsp.
3 mL	salt	½ tsp.

Glaze:

40 g	sweet (unsalted) butter	¼ cup
150 g	brown sugar	¾ cup
45 mL	whipping cream	3 tbsp.

Decoration:

30 g	walnut halves	⅓ cup

Batter:
PREHEAT oven to 180°C (350°F). Grease a 1.5 (8½″ × 4½″) loaf pan.
COMBINE dates and boiling water. Set aside to then drain well.
CREAM butter, sugar, vanilla sugar and egg toge in small mixer bowl until light and fluffy. Stir in walnuts and dates.
SIFT flour, baking powder and salt together over creamed mixture. Mix well.
TURN batter into prepared pan.
BAKE on middle oven rack at 180°C (350°F) for 50-60 minutes.
REMOVE from pan. Let cool.
Glaze:
COMBINE butter, brown sugar and whipping cre in small saucepan. Bring to a boil, stirring consta
BOIL 2 minutes, stirring constantly. Let cool slig stirring occasionally.
POUR glaze evenly over top and sides of cake.
DECORATE with walnut halves.

Recipe No. 467 South Tyr

Tyrolese Apple Ring

Dough:

Metric		Ingredient	Imperial	
500	g	all-purpose flour	3⅓	cups
1	pkg	**oetker** instant dry yeast	1	pkg.
120	g	sugar	½	cup
1	pkg	**oetker** vanilla sugar	1	pkg.
	pinch	salt		pinch
1		egg	1	
120	g	butter or margarine, melted	½	cup
approx 250	mL	lukewarm milk	1	cup

Filling:

Metric		Ingredient	Imperial	
250	g	cream cheese or Quark, softened	1¼	cups
50	g	sugar	¼	cup
5	drops	**oetker** lemon flavouring concentrate	5	drops
1		egg	1	
750	g	apples	1½	lbs.
100	g	sugar	½	cup
1		egg yolk, slightly beaten	1	
50	g	pine nuts or slivered almonds	½	cup

Dough:
PREHEAT oven to 200°C (400°F). Grease and flour baking sheet.
COMBINE flour and yeast in large bowl. Make a wel in centre.
PUT sugar, vanilla sugar, salt, egg and melted butter in well.
WORK flour into centre ingredients, gradually addin milk.
KNEAD dough with dough hooks or by hand until blistered and shiny in appearance and no longer stick about 5 minutes. Place in greased bowl.
LET RISE, covered, in warm place until doubled in size, about 1 hour. Knead again.
ROLL out dough to a 5 mm (¼") thick rectangle.
Filling:
COMBINE cheese, sugar, flavouring concentrate and eg
BEAT until smooth. Spread filling evenly over dough
PEEL and core apples, cut into small pieces.
DISTRIBUTE evenly over filling. Sprinkle with sug
ROLL up dough tightly, starting at long side.
SHAPE roll into a ring on prepared baking sheet.
PRESS ends together to seal.
MAKE incisions at regular intervals on top of dough rin
BRUSH with beaten egg yolk. Sprinkle with pine nu
BAKE on middle oven rack at 200°C (400°F) for 30-40 minutes. Serve warm or cool.

Recipe No. 468 Spai

Banana Souffle a la Oporto

Batter:

Metric		Ingredient	Imperial	
100	g	butter or margarine, softened	½	cup
100	g	sugar	½	cup
2		egg yolks	2	
½	btl	**oetker** lemon flavouring concentrate	½	btl.
4		ripe bananas	4	
100	g	dry bread crumbs	1	cup
50	g	shredded coconut	⅔	cup
60	mL	port wine	¼	cup
250	mL	orange juice	1	cup
2		egg whites	2	

Sauce:

Metric		Ingredient	Imperial	
20	g	**oetker** Gustin cornstarch	2	tbsp.
250	mL	red wine	1	cup
250	mL	water	1	cup
1		cinnamon stick	1	
		sugar to taste		

Batter:
PREHEAT oven to 180°C (350°F). Grease a shallow 2 L (8 cup) casserole.
SPRINKLE with dry bread crumbs.
COMBINE butter, sugar, egg yolks and flavouring concentrate in small mixer bowl.
BEAT at high speed of electric mixer until thick and creamy.
MASH bananas. Gradually add bananas, bread crumbs, shredded coconut, port wine and orange juic to mixture. Mix well.
BEAT egg whites to stiff peaks.
FOLD gently into banana mixture.
TURN into prepared pan.
BAKE on middle oven rack at 180°C (350°F) for 40-50 minutes.
Sauce:
MIX cornstarch and ½ of wine to a smooth consistency.
COMBINE remaining wine, water, cinnamon stick an sugar in small saucepan. Bring to a boil.
STIR cornstarch mixture into saucepan. Bring to a boil, stirring constantly until smoothly thickened. Remove cinnamon stick.
SERVE banana souffle hot or cold together with sauc

Baklava

Pastry:			
2 pkg	frozen puff pastry (397 g/14 oz. each)	2 pkg.	
120 g	butter or margarine, melted	½ cup	
Filling:			
200 g	ground walnuts	2 cups	
150 g	sugar	¾ cup	
Sauce:			
200 mL	liquid honey	⅔ cup	
150 g	sugar	¾ cup	
1	whole lemon, cut in 5 slices	1	
250 mL	water	1 cup	

Pastry:
PREHEAT oven to 180°C (350°F). Grease a shallo casserole or cake pan.
THAW puff pastry according to package directions.
ROLL out pastry thinly. Cut into 10-12 pieces the s of the pan.
PLACE 4 pieces into prepared pan, brushing each piece with melted butter.
Filling:
COMBINE walnuts and sugar. Mix well.
PUT 4 pieces of pastry aside.
PLACE remaining dough pieces in pan, covering ea one evenly with walnut mixture.
PLACE 4 pieces of pastry over walnut mixture, brushing each piece with melted butter.
BAKE on middle oven rack at 180°C (350°F) for 30-40 minutes.
Sauce:
COMBINE honey, sugar, lemon slices and water in small saucepan. Bring to a boil, then simmer 5 minutes. Remove lemon slices.
POUR ½ of sauce over baked Baklava. Let cool.
POUR remaining sauce over Baklava just before serving.

Recipe No. 470 Ita

Cassata Parfait

Candied almonds:

50 g	sugar	¼ cup
50 g	chopped almonds	½ cup

Ingredients:

70 g	candied chopped almonds (see above)	¾ cup
50 g	pistachios, chopped	½ cup
50 g	walnuts, chopped	½ cup
50 g	candied cherries	½ cup
15 mL	liquid honey	1 tbsp.
45 mL	cognac or brandy	3 tbsp.
5	egg yolks	5
150 g	sugar	¾ cup
500 mL	whipping cream	2 cups

Decoration:

shaved chocolate

Candied almonds:
GREASE a baking sheet.
HEAT sugar in small saucepan until melted and golden brown.
ADD almonds. Toast lightly, stirring to coat nuts in syrup.
REMOVE from heat and pour immediately onto prepared baking sheet.
COOL. Chop into small pieces.

Method:
COMBINE candied almonds, pistachios, walnuts an candied cherries. Mix well.
ADD honey and cognac to nut mixture. Mix well.
COMBINE egg yolks and sugar in top of double boil
BEAT over simmering water until thick and creamy. Let cool.
ADD to nut mixture. Mix well.
BEAT whipping cream to stiff peaks.
FOLD into nut mixture, gently but thoroughly.
TURN into desired pan.
FREEZE until firm, 4 hours or overnight.
DIP pan quickly into hot water to unmould. Turn upside down onto serving plate.
DECORATE with shaved chocolate.
SERVE immediately.

Recipe No. 471 Engla

London Meringue Slices

Pastry:

250 g	all-purpose flour	1⅔ cups
1 pkg	**oetker** baking powder (14 g/4 tsp)	1 pkg.
2 pkg	**oetker** vanilla sugar	2 pkg.
4	egg yolks	4
150 g	butter or margarine, cold	¾ cup

Filling:

200 g	apricot jam, marmalade or raspberry jam	1 cup

Meringue:

4	egg whites	4
200 g	sugar	1 cup
100 g	raisins	1 cup
60 g	ground hazelnuts or almonds	⅔ cup
5 drops	**oetker** lemon flavouring concentrate	5 drops

Pastry:
PREHEAT oven to 180°C (350°F). Grease a baking sheet.
SIFT flour and baking powder onto pastry board. Make a well in centre.
PUT vanilla sugar and egg yolks in well. Work a litt flour into centre to make a stiff dough.
CUT cold butter into small pieces over flour mixtur
WORK all ingredients together quickly to make a smooth dough.
ROLL out or press pastry to 5 mm (¼″) thickness onto prepared baking sheet. Prick dough with fork several times.
BAKE on middle oven rack at 180°C (350°F) for 10-15 minutes, or until light golden.
SPREAD jam evenly over pastry.

Meringue:
BEAT egg whites to soft peaks. Gradually add sugar beating to stiff peaks.
FOLD raisins, hazelnuts and flavouring concentrate carefully into meringue.
SPREAD evenly over jam.
BAKE on middle oven rack at 180°C (350°F) for 10-15 minutes.
COOL completely.
CUT into diamonds or bars to serve.

SWEET BIT

& BITES

Recipe No. 472 Swed

Swedish Vanilla Balls

Filling:

1 pkg	**oetker** vanilla pudding powder	1 pkg.
50 g	sugar	¼ cup
500 mL	milk	2 cups

Dough:

500 g	all-purpose flour	3⅓ cups
1 pkg	**oetker** instant dry yeast	1 pkg.
80 g	sugar	⅓ cup
5 mL	ground cinnamon	1 tsp.
pinch	salt	pinch
1	egg yolk	1
100 g	butter or margarine, melted	½ cup
approx 250 mL	lukewarm milk	1 cup

Decoration:

100 g	icing sugar, sifted	½ cup
	butter or margarine, melted	

Filling:
PREPARE pudding according to package directions.
LET COOL, stirring occasionally.
Dough:
PREHEAT oven to 200°C (400°F). Grease a baking she
COMBINE flour and yeast in large bowl. Make a we in centre.
PUT sugar, cinnamon, salt, egg yolk and melted butt in well.
WORK flour into centre ingredients, gradually addin milk.
KNEAD dough with dough hooks or by hand until blistered and shiny in appearance and no longer stick about 5 minutes.
PLACE in greased bowl.
LET RISE, covered, in warm place until doubled in size, about 1 hour.
KNEAD again.
ROLL out dough to 5 mm (¼") thickness.
CUT into 7 cm (2¾") rounds with floured cutter.
SPREAD pudding evenly on ½ of dough rounds.
PLACE remaining rounds on top. Press seams firmly together to seal.
PLACE onto prepared baking sheet.
COVER with a cloth and let rise 30 minutes.
BAKE on middle oven rack at 200°C (400°F) for 10-15 minutes.
BRUSH with melted butter while still warm.
SPRINKLE with icing sugar.

Recipe No. 473 Ita

Love Knots

Dough:

300 g	all-purpose flour	2 cups
½ pkg	**oetker** baking powder (7 g/2 tsp)	½ pkg.
100 g	sugar	½ cup
1 pkg	**oetker** natural vanilla sugar	1 pkg.
5 mL	ground anise	1 tsp.
75 mL	whipping cream	⅓ cup
1	egg	1
1	egg yolk	1
80 g	butter or margarine, cold	⅓ cup

Glaze:

150 g	icing sugar, sifted	1 cup
15 mL	hot water	1 tbsp.
15 mL	cherry liqueur	1 tbsp.

Dough:
PREHEAT oven to 200°C (400°F). Line a baking sheet with parchment paper.
SIFT flour and baking powder onto pastry board. Make a well in centre.
PUT sugar, vanilla sugar, anise, whipping cream, egg and egg yolk in well. Work a little flour into centre mixture to make a stiff dough.
CUT cold butter into small pieces over mixture.
WORK all ingredients together quickly to make a smooth dough.
CHILL slightly for easy rolling, about 30 minutes.
ROLL out dough on floured surface to 5 mm (¼") thickness.
CUT into 10 cm (4") long strips.
TWIST loosely into knots; see photo.
PLACE onto prepared baking sheet.
BAKE on middle oven rack at 200°C (400°F) for 12-18 minutes.
Glaze:
COMBINE icing sugar, water and cherry liqueur to make a thick glaze consistency.
SPREAD over Love Knots.

Recipe No. 474 Spa

Almond Rum Squares

Dough:

300 g	all-purpose flour	2 cups
½ pkg	**oetker** baking powder (7 g/2 tsp)	½ pkg.
200 g	sugar	1 cup
1 pkg	**oetker** natural vanilla sugar	1 pkg.
pinch	salt	pinch
15 mL	rum	1 tbsp.
3	eggs	3
180 g	butter or margarine, cold	¾ cup
1	egg yolk, slightly beaten	1

Decoration:

60 g	chopped almonds	½ cup

Glaze:

60 mL	rum	¼ cup
	icing sugar, sifted	

Dough:
PREHEAT oven to 190°C (375°F). Grease a baking sheet.
SIFT flour and baking powder onto pastry board. make a well in centre.
PUT sugar, vanilla sugar, salt, rum and eggs in well. Work a little flour into centre to make a stiff dough.
CUT cold butter into small pieces over mixture.
WORK all ingredients together quickly to make a smooth dough.
CHILL slightly for easy rolling, about 1 hour.
ROLL out dough on floured surface to about 3 mm (⅛″) thickness.
CUT into rectangles or as desired.
PLACE onto prepared baking sheet.
BRUSH with beaten egg yolk. Sprinkle with almonc
BAKE on middle oven rack at 190°C (375°F) for 8-15 minutes. Cool.
Glaze:
COMBINE rum and enough icing sugar to make a glaze consistency. Drizzle over cookies.

Recipe No. 475 Swed

Swedish Apple Tarts

Pastry:

250 g	all-purpose flour	1⅔ cups
80 g	shortening, softened	⅓ cup
130 g	butter or margarine, softened	⅔ cup
pinch	salt	pinch
90-120 mL	water	6-8 tbsp.

Filling:

750 g	apples	1½ lbs.
250 mL	water	1 cup
50 g	chopped almonds	½ cup
50 g	ground almonds	½ cup
1 btl	**oetker** rum flavouring concentrate	1 btl.
30 mL	cognac or brandy	2 tbsp.

Decoration:

	icing sugar, sifted	
50 g	semi-sweet chocolate, melted	2 sq.

Pastry:
PREHEAT oven to 180°C (350°F). Grease 15-18 fluted tart pans.
SIFT flour onto pastry board. Make a well in centre
PUT shortening, butter, salt and water in well.
WORK all ingredients together quickly to make a smooth dough.
CHILL slightly for easy rolling, about 1 hour.
ROLL out ⅔ of pastry on floured surface to 2 mm (⅛″) thickness.
CUT out rounds with a floured cutter 9 cm (3½″) ir diameter. Fit into prepared tart pans. Press pastry down firmly in pans.
Filling:
PEEL and core apples. Cut into small pieces.
COMBINE apples and water in saucepan. Cook to make applesauce. Add almonds, rum flavouring and cognac. Mix well. Let cool.
SPOON about 15 mL (1 tbsp.) mixture onto pastry.
ROLL out remaining pastry on floured surface to 2 n (⅛″) thickness.
CUT out rounds with a floured cutter to fit tart pan
PLACE over apple mixture. Press edges together to s
BRUSH tops with cold water. Bake on middle oven rack at 180°C (350°F) for 30-35 minutes.
REMOVE from tart pans. Place on baking sheet.
BAKE at 180°C (350°F) for 5-10 minutes. Let cool completely.
SPRINKLE with icing sugar. Decorate with chocola

Recipe No. 476 Fran

French Meringue

Meringue:

8	egg whites	8
250 g	sugar	1¼ cups
200 g	icing sugar, sifted	1⅓ cups
1 pkg	**oetker** baking powder	1 pkg.

Filling:

500 mL	vanilla ice cream, sherbet or kiwi ice	2 cups
5	kiwi fruit	5

Decoration:

250 mL	whipping cream	1 cup
1 pkg	**oetker** Whip-it	1 pkg.
1 pkg	**oetker** vanilla sugar	1 pkg.

Method:

PREHEAT oven to 120°C (250°F). Line baking shee with parchment paper.
BEAT egg whites to soft peaks. Gradually add sugar beating to stiff peaks.
SIFT icing sugar and baking powder over egg white mixture. Fold in gently but thoroughly.
FILL mixture into decorating bag.
PIPE 5 cm (2″) rounds onto prepared baking sheet.
BAKE on middle oven rack at 120°C (250°F) for 1 hour.
TURN oven off and leave meringues in oven 1½ hou longer.

Decoration:

BEAT whipping cream to soft peaks. Gradually add Whip-it and vanilla sugar, beating to stiff peaks.
FILL half of meringues with vanilla ice cream, sherb or kiwi ice. Top with another meringue and decorate with kiwi slices and whipped cream.

Recipe No. 477 Fran

Cream Filled Profiteroles

Dough:

250 mL	water	1 cup
pinch	salt	pinch
100 g	butter or margarine	½ cup
25 g	sugar	2 tbsp.
150 g	all-purpose flour	1 cup
3-4	eggs	3-4
5 mL	**oetker** baking powder	1 tsp.

Filling:

75 mL	milk	⅓ cup
3	egg yolks	3
100 g	sugar	½ cup
1 pkg	**oetker** vanilla sugar	1 pkg.
10 g	**oetker** cornstarch	1 tbsp.
250 mL	whipping cream	1 cup

Chocolate Sauce:

1 pkg	**oetker** Chocofix	1 pkg.
	OR	
150 g	semi-sweet chocolate, chopped	6 sq.
75 mL	whipping cream	⅓ cup

Dough:

PREHEAT oven to 200°C (400°F). Grease and flour baking sheet.
COMBINE water, salt, butter and sugar in a saucepa Bring to a boil. Remove from heat.
ADD flour all at once. Cook, stirring vigorously unti mixture leaves sides of pan, about 1 minute.
REMOVE from heat. Turn into mixing bowl.
ADD eggs, one at a time, beating well after each addition until smooth and shiny. Let Cool.
STIR in baking powder thoroughly.
DROP batter by spoonfuls in 5 cm (2″) rounds onto prepared baking sheet OR squeeze through a decorating bag with large round tube.
BAKE on middle oven rack at 200°C (400°F) for about 40 minutes. Do not open oven door during fir 15 minutes baking.
CUT off tops immediately after baking. Let cool.

Filling:

BRING milk to a boil.
BEAT egg yolks, sugar, vanilla sugar and cornstarch together. Add slowly to boiling milk, stirring constantly. Boil for 1 minute. Let cool.
BEAT whipping cream to stiff peaks.
FOLD into egg mixture, gently but thoroughly.
FILL into decorating bag. Fill bottom of puffs with cream mixture.

Chocolate Sauce:

SOFTEN Chocofix as directed on package, OR COMBINE chocolate and whipping cream in top of double boiler.
HEAT over simmering water, stirring until melted.
POUR evenly over tops. Let chocolate set.
PLACE tops over filling.

Recipe No. 478 Engla

Brandy Snaps

Pastry:

75 g	butter or margarine	⅓ cup
100 g	sugar	½ cup
100 g	corn syrup	⅓ cup
½ btl	**oetker** lemon flavouring concentrate	½ btl.
190 g	all-purpose flour	1¼ cups
2 mL	ginger	½ tsp.
45 mL	cognac or brandy	3 tbsp.

Filling:

250 mL	whipping cream	1 cup
1 pkg	**oetker** Whip-it	1 pkg.
1 pkg	**oetker** vanilla sugar	1 pkg.
45 mL	cognac or brandy	3 tbsp.

Decoration:

50 g	semi-sweet chocolate, melted	2 sq.

Pastry:
PREHEAT oven to 190°C (375°F). Grease a baking sheet.
COMBINE butter, sugar, syrup and flavouring concentrate in saucepan. Heat, stirring constantly, t dissolve sugar. Remove from heat.
ADD flour, ginger and cognac. Stir well until smoo
PLACE 20 mL (4 tsp.) dough for each cookie onto prepared baking sheet, allowing room to spread.
BAKE on middle oven rack at 190°C (375°F) for 6- minutes. Cool slightly.
WRAP around greased sticks 2 cm (¾″) diameter to form hollow tubes. If cookies become too cool to ro rewarm slightly in oven.
Filling:
BEAT whipping cream to soft peaks. Gradually add Whip-it and vanilla sugar. Beat to stiff peaks.
ADD cognac. Mix gently but thoroughly.
DECORATE one end of cookies with melted chocolate. Let set. Fill with whipped cream mixture.

Recipe No. 479 Fran

Croissants

Dough:

500 g	all-purpose flour	3⅓ cups
1 pkg	**oetker** instant dry yeast	1 pkg.
5 mL	salt	1 tsp.
60 g	sugar	⅓ cup
approx 250 mL	lukewarm milk	1 cup

Butter "Brick":

200 g	butter, softened	1 cup
50 g	all-purpose flour	⅓ cup

Decoration:

1	egg yolk, slightly beaten	1
30 mL	milk	2 tbsp.
5 mL	icing sugar	1 tsp.
	finely chopped almonds or sesame seeds, optional	

Dough:
PREHEAT oven to 200°C (400°F). Grease a baking sheet.
COMBINE flour and yeast in large bowl. Make a w in centre. Put salt, sugar and milk into well.
KNEAD dough with dough hooks or by hand, until smooth, elastic and blistered in appearance, about 5 minutes. Cover with a cloth and let rise in warm pla until doubled in size, about 1 hour.
Butter "Brick":
COMBINE soft butter and flour until smooth. Shap into a "brick" (20 × 10 cm/8″ × 4″). Chill until fi
ROLL dough into a rectangle (30 × 25 cm/12″ × 1
PLACE brick in middle of dough rectangle.
BRUSH sides of dough lightly with water.
FOLD dough over butter "brick" and press sides together. The butter has to be completely wrapped i the dough. Carefully roll out rectangle (30 × 40 cm 12″ × 16″). Fold narrow sides of dough into centre (folding a towel) to create three layers. Chill 30 minut
REPEAT rolling and folding 2-3 times.
ROLL out dough on floured surface to a rectangle (60 cm × 30 cm/24″ × 12″). Cut out squares 15 cm 15 cm (6″ × 6″). Cut squares into halves, forming triangles.
MAKE 3 cm (1″) incisions at long side of triangles.
ROLL up starting at long side. Shape into crescents
LET RISE, covered, in warm place, 30-40 minutes.
BRUSH with mixture of egg yolk, milk and icing sug
SPRINKLE with chopped almonds or sesame seeds desired. Place onto prepared baking sheet.
BAKE on middle oven rack at 200°C (400°F) for 12-15 minutes.

Bananas in Blankets

Dough:

250 g	all-purpose flour	1⅔ cups
1 pkg	**oetker** vanilla sugar	1 pkg.
pinch	salt	pinch
60 mL	cold water	¼ cup
130 g	butter or margarine, cold	⅔ cup

Filling:

6	bananas	6
	sugar	
1	egg, slightly beaten	1

Decoration:

125 mL	whipping cream	½ cup
1 pkg	**oetker** Whip-it	1 pkg.
1 pkg	**oetker** vanilla sugar	1 pkg.

Dough:
PREHEAT oven to 190°C (375°F). Grease a baking sheet.
SIFT flour onto pastry board. Make a well in centre.
PUT vanilla sugar, salt and water in well. Work a lit flour into centre mixture to make a stiff dough.
CUT cold butter into small pieces over mixture.
WORK all ingredients together quickly to make a smooth dough.
CHILL slightly for easy rolling, about 30 minutes.
ROLL out dough on floured surface to about 5 mm (¼″) thickness.
CUT into 6 rectangles.
Filling:
PEEL bananas. Roll in sugar.
WRAP bananas in dough rectangles. Seal seams well
BRUSH with beaten egg.
PLACE onto prepared baking sheet.
BAKE on middle oven rack at 190°C (375°F) for 20-25 minutes.
Decoration:
BEAT whipping cream to soft peaks. Gradually add Whip-it and vanilla sugar, beating to stiff peaks.
DECORATE attractively.

Chocolate Croissants

Dough:
See recipe no. 479 (Croissants)

Filling:

200 g	semi-sweet chocolate bar, cut into long fingers	7 oz.
1	egg yolk, slightly beaten	1
30 mL	milk	2 tbsp.
5 mL	icing sugar	1 tsp.

Dough:
PREHEAT oven to 225°C (450°F). Grease a baking sheet.
PREPARE dough, using ingredients and method in recipe no. 479.
ROLL out dough to about 3 mm (⅛″) thickness.
CUT out rectangles 9 × 12 cm (3″ × 5″).
PLACE one long piece of chocolate onto each rectang
COMBINE beaten egg yolk, milk and icing sugar. M well.
BRUSH sides of dough with egg mixture.
ROLL up dough from long side.
PLACE onto prepared baking sheet.
LET RISE, covered, in warm place, 30-40 minutes.
BRUSH surface of rolls with egg mixture.
BAKE on middle oven rack at 225°C (450°F) for 15-20 minutes.

Recipe No. 482 Germa

Liegnitz Special

Batter:

120 g	sugar	½ cup	
175 mL	liquid honey	⅔ cup	
60 g	butter or margarine	⅓ cup	
15 mL	whipping cream	1 tbsp.	
2	eggs	2	
½ btl	**oetker** lemon flavouring concentrate	½ btl.	
5 mL	ground cinnamon	1 tsp.	
2 mL	ground cloves	½ tsp.	
dash	ground nutmeg	dash	
30 g	cocoa	⅓ cup	
60 g	raisins	½ cup	
60 g	chopped candied orange peel	½ cup	
60 g	chopped almonds	½ cup	
250 g	all-purpose flour	1⅔ cups	
½ pkg	**oetker** baking powder (7 g/2 tsp)	½ pkg.	

Filling:

200 g	apricot jam or marmalade, strained	1 cup

Glaze:

250 g	semi-sweet chocolate, melted	10 sq.

Batter:
PREHEAT oven to 180°C (350°F). Line muffin cup with paper baking cups.
COMBINE sugar, honey, butter and whipping crean in saucepan.
HEAT, stirring constantly, to dissolve sugar.
REMOVE from heat. Let cool.
ADD eggs, flavouring concentrate, spices and cocoa Stir well.
ADD raisins, candied orange peel and almonds.
SIFT flour and baking powder over mixture. Fold i gently but thoroughly.
TURN batter into paper baking cups.
BAKE on middle oven rack at 180°C (350°F) for 15-20 minutes.
REMOVE paper cups immediately.
SPREAD top and sides of cakes with jam. Let cool.
SPREAD top and sides with melted chocolate.
DECORATE attractively with chocolate, if desired; see photo.

Recipe No. 483 Engla

Tiger Cakes

Dough:

120 g	all-purpose flour	¾ cup
150 g	sugar	¾ cup
1 pkg	**oetker** vanilla sugar	1 pkg.
100 g	butter or margarine, cold	½ cup

Coffee Creme Filling:

100 g	butter or margarine, softened	½ cup
120 g	sugar	½ cup
5 mL	instant coffee powder	1 tsp.

Decoration:

50 g	chopped walnuts or pecans	½ cup

Glaze:

75 g	sugar	⅓ cup
45 mL	water	3 tbsp.

Dough:
PREHEAT oven to 200°C (400°F). Grease a bakin sheet.
SIFT flour onto pastry board. Make a well in centr
PUT sugar and vanilla sugar in well.
CUT cold butter into small pieces over flour.
WORK all ingredients together quickly to make a smooth dough.
CHILL slightly for easy rolling, about ½ hour.
CUT into 5 cm (2″) rounds with floured cutter.
PLACE onto prepared baking sheet.
BAKE on middle oven rack at 200°C (400°F) for 8-10 minutes. Let cool.

Filling:
BEAT butter, sugar and coffee powder at high spee of electric mixer until thick and creamy.
SPREAD some of cream mixture on half of cookies Cover with remaining cookies.
SPREAD remaining cream mixture on sides of cook Sprinkle sides with walnuts.
MELT sugar in small saucepan over low heat until caramel colour. Gradually add water, stirring constar
DRIZZLE warm syrup over tops of cookies.

NOTE: Cookies can also be filled with whipped cr or a vanilla creme filling.

Recipe No. 484 — Fran[cel]

Almond Tarts

Pastry:

1 pkg	frozen puff pastry (397 g/14 oz.)	1 pkg.

Filling:

1	egg	1
60 mL	milk	¼ cup
30 mL	rum	2 tbsp.
	grated rind of 1 orange	
120 g	ground almonds	1¼ cups
100 g	sugar	½ cup

Decoration:

	whole blanched almonds	
40 g	icing sugar, sifted	⅓ cup

Pastry:
PREHEAT oven to 220°C (425°F). Rinse 12 fluted tart pans with cold water.
THAW puff pastry according to package directions.
ROLL out pastry on floured surface to 3 mm (⅛″) thickness.
CUT out twelve 10 cm (4″) rounds with floured cutt[er].
FIT into prepared tart pans.
Filling:
COMBINE egg, milk, rum and orange rind. Gradual[ly] add ground almonds and sugar. Mix well.
SPOON mixture into pastry.
DECORATE with whole almonds. Sprinkle with icin[g] sugar.
BAKE on middle oven rack at 220°C (425°F) for 15-20 minutes.

Recipe No. 485 — Spa[in]

Sevillanos

Batter:

4	egg yolks	4
100 g	sugar	½ cup
1 pkg	**oetker** vanilla sugar	1 pkg.
45 mL	sherry	3 tbsp.
4	egg whites	4
100 g	ground almonds	1 cup
50 g	all-purpose flour	⅓ cup
10 mL	**oetker** baking powder	2 tsp.

Syrup:

75 mL	sherry	⅓ cup
100 g	sugar	½ cup

Batter:
PREHEAT oven to 190°C (375°F). Grease a loaf pa[n].
CREAM egg yolks, ⅔ of sugar and vanilla sugar together in small mixer bowl until light and fluffy. Gradually add sherry.
BEAT egg whites and remaining sugar to stiff peaks.
SIFT flour and baking powder together over egg yol[k] mixture.
SPRINKLE almonds over flour mixture.
FOLD in gently but thoroughly.
FOLD in egg whites.
TURN into prepared loaf pan.
BAKE on middle oven rack at 190°C (375°F) for 25-30 minutes. Let cool. Remove from pan. Slice.
Syrup:
HEAT sherry and sugar together stirring constantly until sugar is dissolved.
POUR over slices.

Recipe No. 486 England

Easter Biscuits

Dough:

250 g	all-purpose flour	1⅔ cups	
130 g	sugar	1 cup	
1 pkg	**oetker** vanilla sugar	1 pkg.	
pinch	salt	pinch	
5 drops	**oetker** lemon flavouring concentrate	5 drops	
2	egg yolks	2	
150 g	butter or margarine, cold	¾ cup	
80 g	raisins	¾ cup	
2	egg whites, slightly beaten	2	

Decoration:

50 g	sugar	¼ cup

Dough:

PREHEAT oven to 180°C (350°F). Grease a baking sheet.
SIFT flour onto pastry board. Make a well in centre.
PUT sugar, vanilla sugar, salt, flavouring concentrate and egg yolks in well.
WORK a little of flour into centre mixture to make a stiff dough.
CUT cold butter into small pieces over flour mixture.
WORK all ingredients together quickly to make a smooth dough.
ADD raisins.
CHILL slightly for easy rolling, about 30 minutes.
ROLL out dough on a lightly floured surface to 3 mm (⅛") thickness.
CUT dough into diamonds.
BRUSH with slightly beaten egg whites.
SPRINKLE with sugar.
PLACE onto prepared baking sheet.
BAKE on middle oven rack at 180°C (350°F) for 10-15 minutes.

Recipe No. 487 Yugoslav

Belgrade Tea Cookies

Batter:

3	eggs	3
250 g	sugar	1¼ cups
5 mL	ground cinnamon	1 tsp.
5 drops	**oetker** lemon flavouring concentrate	5 drops
250 g	chopped almonds	2½ cups
30 g	chopped candied orange peel	¼ cup
180 g	all-purpose flour	1¼ cups
pinch	**oetker** baking powder	pinch

Batter:

PREHEAT oven to 200°C (400°F). Grease and flour a baking sheet.
BEAT eggs and sugar at high speed of electric mixer until thick and creamy. Stir in cinnamon, flavouring concentrate, almonds and candied orange peel. Mix well.
SIFT flour and baking powder together over egg mixture.
FOLD in gently but thoroughly.
DROP by tablespoonful onto prepared baking sheet.
BAKE on middle oven rack at 200°C (400°F) for 9-12 minutes.

NOTE: To store, place with small pieces of apple in tin or container with tight fitting lid.

Recipe No. 488 Australi[a]

Scones

Dough:

250	all purpose flour	1⅔ cups
10 mL	**oetker** baking powder	2 tsp.
2 mL	salt	½ tsp.
125 mL	milk	½ cup
30 g	butter or margarine, cold	2 tbsp.
45 mL	milk	3 tbsp.

Filling:

100 g	strawberry jam or marmalade	½ cup
250 mL	whipping cream	1 cup
1 pkg	**oetker** Whip-it	1 pkg.
1 pkg	**oetker** vanilla sugar	1 pkg.

Dough:
PREHEAT oven to 225°C (450°F). Grease a baking sheet.
SIFT flour and baking powder together onto pastry board. Make a well in centre.
PUT salt and milk in well.
WORK a little flour into centre mixture to make a stif[f] dough.
CUT cold butter into small pieces over mixture.
WORK all ingredients together quickly to make a smooth dough.
CHILL slightly for easy rolling, about 20 minutes.
ROLL out dough on floured surface to 2 cm (¾″) thickness.
CUT into 5 cm (2″) rounds with floured cutter.
BRUSH with milk.
PLACE onto prepared baking sheet.
BAKE on middle oven rack at 225°C (450°F) for 8-12 minutes.
CUT rounds horizontally into two layers.
Filling:
SPREAD jam over bottom layers.
BEAT whipping cream to soft peaks. Gradually add Whip-it and vanilla sugar, beating to stiff peaks.
SPOON or pipe whipped cream onto jam.
PLACE top layers onto whipping cream mixture. Serv[e] warm or cold.

Recipe No. 489 Greec[e]

Greek Almond Rolls

Pastry:

1 pkg	frozen puff pastry (397 g/14 oz.)	1 pkg.

Filling:

120 g	ground almonds	1¼ cups
60 g	sugar	⅓ cup
1	egg	1

Syrup:

250 mL	water	1 cup
120 g	sugar	⅔ cup
½ btl	**oetker** lemon flavouring concentrate	½ btl.
1	cinnamon stick	1

Pastry:
PREHEAT oven to 190°C (375°F). Grease a baking sheet.
THAW puff pastry according to package directions.
ROLL out pastry on floured surface to 5 mm (¼″) thickness.
CUT into 4 × 20 cm (1½″ × 8″) rectangles.
Filling:
COMBINE ground almonds, sugar and egg. Mix well.
PLACE about 5 mL (1 tsp.) of filling onto each rectangle.
ROLL up evenly from short end.
PLACE onto prepared baking sheet.
BAKE on middle oven rack at 190°C (375°F) for 20-30 minutes.
Syrup:
COMBINE all ingredients in small saucepan. Bring t[o] a boil, then simmer for 5-10 minutes.
DIP pastry into hot syrup. Let cool.

Recipe No. 490 Engla

Glazed Ginger Hearts

Dough:

200	g	all-purpose flour	1⅓ cups
1	pkg	**oetker** baking powder	1 pkg.
120	g	sugar	½ cup
1	pkg	**oetker** vanilla sugar	1 pkg.
	pinch	salt	pinch
5	mL	ginger	1 tsp.
1		egg	1
120	g	butter or margarine, cold	½ cup

Glaze:

1	pkg	**oetker** Chocofix	1 pkg.
		OR	
100	g	semi-sweet chocolate	4 sq.
50	g	sweet (unsalted) butter	¼ cup

Decoration:

coarse sugar sprinkles

Dough:
PREHEAT oven to 190°C (375°F). Grease a baking sheet.
SIFT flour and baking powder onto pastry board. Make a well in cenre.
PUT sugar, vanilla sugar, salt, ginger and egg in wel
Mix small amount of flour mixture into centre ingredients to make a stiff dough.
CUT cold butter into small pieces over flour.
WORK all ingredients together quickly to make a smooth dough.
CHILL for about 2 hours.
ROLL out dough on lightly floured surface to 5 mm (¼″) thickness.
CUT into hearts or desired shapes with floured cutt
PLACE onto prepared baking sheet.
BAKE at 190°C (375°F) for 12-15 minutes. Let coo

Glaze:
SOFTEN Chocofix as directed on package OR
COMBINE chocolate and butter in top of double boiler.
PLACE over simmering water, stirring until melted.
SPREAD evenly over hearts.
SPRINKLE with sugar.

Recipe No. 491 Hunga

Coconut Kisses

Batter:

4		egg whites	4
240	g	icing sugar, sifted	2 cups
1	pkg	**oetker** vanilla sugar	1 pkg.
100	g	shredded coconut	1¼ cups
100	g	all-purpose flour	⅔ cup

Batter:
PREHEAT oven to 120°C (250°F). Grease a baking sheet. Line with parchment or waxed paper.
BEAT egg whites to soft peaks. Gradually add icing sugar and vanilla sugar, beating to stiff peaks.
FOLD in coconut, gently but thoroughly.
PLACE mixture in saucepan. Heat to about 80°C (175°F), stirring constantly. Do not boil.
REMOVE from heat.
STIR flour into mixture.
PUT mixture in decorating bag with large star tube.
SQUEEZE onto prepared baking sheet.
BAKE on middle oven rack at 120°C (250°F) for 50-60 minutes.

Romanian Chocolate Cupcakes

Ingredients:

2	egg whites, unbeaten	2
250 g	chopped almonds	2½ cups
250 g	icing sugar, sifted	1⅔ cups
100 g	semi-sweet chocolate, grated	4 sq.
1	egg, slightly beaten, optional	1

Method:

PREHEAT oven to 150°C (300°F). Line muffin cup with paper baking cups.
COMBINE egg whites, chopped almonds, icing suga and grated chocolate. Mix well.
SPOON into paper baking cups, filling half full.
BRUSH with beaten egg, if desired.
BAKE on middle oven rack at 150°C (300°F) for 45-60 minutes.

Chocolate Kisses

Ingredients:

100 g	butter or margarine, softened	½ cup
200 g	semi-sweet chocolate, grated	8 sq.
100 g	icing sugar, sifted	⅔ cup
100 g	ground almonds	1 cup
6	egg whites	6

Filling:

375 mL	whipping cream	1½ cups
1 pkg	**oetker** Whip-it	1 pkg.
1 pkg	**oetker** vanilla sugar	1 pkg.

Decoration:

50 g	semi-sweet chocolate, melted	2 sq.

Method:

PREHEAT oven to 190°C (375°F). Line muffin cup with paper baking cups.
CREAM butter, chocolate, icing sugar and ground almonds together in mixing bowl until light.
BEAT egg whites to stiff peaks.
FOLD into chocolate mixture, gently but thoroughly
SPOON into paper baking cups, filling half full.
BAKE on middle oven rack at 190°C (375°F) for 18-25 minutes.
REMOVE from paper cups immediately. Let cool.
SLICE in half horizontally to make 2 layers.

Filling:

BEAT whipping cream to soft peaks. Gradually add Whip-it and vanilla sugar, beating to stiff peaks.
PIPE whipped cream on bottom layers.
COVER with top layers.
DRIZZLE melted chocolate over top layers.

Russian Cheese Rounds

Dough:

500 g	all-purpose flour	3⅓ cups	
1 pkg	**oetker** instant dry yeast	1 pkg.	
50 g	sugar	¼ cup	
pinch	salt	pinch	
30 mL	vegetable oil	2 tbsp.	
325 mL	lukewarm milk	1¼ cups	

Filling:

130 g	cottage cheese, Quark or ricotta	¾ cup
1	egg yolk	1
30 g	sugar	2 tbsp.
50 g	raisins	½ cup
5 drops	**oetker** lemon flavouring concentrate	5 drops
1	egg, slightly beaten	1

Dough:
PREHEAT oven to 200°C (400°F). Grease a baking sheet.
COMBINE flour and yeast in large mixing bowl. Ma a well in centre.
PUT sugar, salt and oil in well.
WORK flour into centre ingredients, gradually addin milk.
KNEAD dough with dough hooks or by hand until smooth, elastic and no longer sticky, about 5 minutes
LET RISE, covered, in warm place, about 40 minute
KNEAD again.
ROLL out dough to 1 cm (½″) thickness.
CUT into 7 cm (3″) rounds with floured cutter.
MAKE a well in centre of each round.
Filling:
COMBINE all ingredients. Mix well.
SPOON filling into well of each round.
PLACE onto prepared baking sheet.
LET RISE, covered, for about 20 minutes.
BRUSH with beaten egg.
BAKE on middle oven rack at 200°C (400°F) for 15-25 minutes.
SERVE warm or cool.

Choco Delights

Ingredients:

200 g	ground almonds	2 cups
100 g	sugar	½ cup
100 g	semi-sweet chocolate, melted	4 sq.
3 mL	instant coffee powder	¾ tsp.
10 mL	hot water	2 tsp.
2	egg whites, slightly beaten	2

Decoration:
blanched whole almonds

Method:
PREHEAT oven to 150°C (300°F). Grease a baking sheet.
COMBINE ground almonds, sugar and melted chocolate. Mix well.
DISSOLVE coffee powder in water.
MIX with slightly beaten egg whites.
ADD to chocolate mixture. Mix well.
SHAPE into small balls.
PLACE onto prepared baking sheet.
PRESS an almond into centre of each cookie.
BAKE on middle oven rack at 150°C (300°F) for 10-15 minutes.
LET stand, covered, overnight.

DEEP FRIE

DELIGHTS

Filled Doughnuts

Dough:

500 g	all-purpose flour	$3\frac{1}{3}$ cups	
1 pkg	**oetker** instant dry yeast	1 pkg.	
80 g	sugar	½ cup	
1 pkg	**oetker** vanilla sugar	1 pkg.	
½ btl	**oetker** lemon flavouring concentrate	½ btl.	
pinch	salt	pinch	
45 mL	rum	3 tbsp.	
4	egg yolks	4	
80 g	butter or margarine, melted	⅓ cup	
approx 250 mL	lukewarm milk	1 cup	

Filling:

70 g	raisins	⅔ cup
70 g	chopped figs	⅔ cup
7	whole dates, chopped	7
100 g	chopped hazelnuts	1 cup
60 mL	apricot jam or marmalade	¼ cup

For deep frying:
oil or shortening

Decoration:
icing sugar, sifted

Dough:
COMBINE flour and yeast in large mixing bowl. Ma
a well in centre.
PUT sugar, vanilla sugar, flavouring concentrate, salt
rum, egg yolks and melted butter into well.
WORK flour into centre ingredients, gradually addin
milk.
KNEAD dough with dough hooks or by hand until smooth, elastic and no longer sticky, about 5 minute
LET RISE, covered, in warm place until doubled in size, about 30 minutes.
KNEAD again.
ROLL out dough on floured surface to about 5 mm (¼″) thickness.
CUT into 5 cm (3″) rounds with floured cutter.

Filling:
COMBINE all ingredients. Mix well.
PLACE filling on half of rounds.
COVER with remaining rounds. Press edges together firmly to seal.
HEAT oil to 190°C (375°F). Keep at an even temperature.
FRY doughnuts, a few at a time, until golden brown on both sides.
REMOVE from oil. Drain on paper towelling. Let cool.
SPRINKLE with icing sugar.

Apricot Fritters

Dough:

200 g	all-purpose flour	$1\frac{1}{3}$ cups
125 mL	milk	½ cup
2	egg yolks	2
45 mL	brandy	3 tbsp.
5 mL	vegetable oil	1 tsp.
pinch	salt	pinch
2	egg whites	2
50 g	sugar	¼ cup
500 g	apricot halves, canned or steamed, well drained	1 lb.

For deep frying:
oil or shortening

Decoration:
sugar
ground cinnamon

Batter:
COMBINE flour, milk, egg yolks, brandy, oil and sa
in large mixing bowl. Mix well until smooth.
BEAT egg whites and sugar to stiff peaks.
FOLD into flour mixture, gently but thoroughly.
HEAT oil to 190°C (375°F). Keep at an even temperature.
DIP apricot halves into batter.
FRY, a few at a time, until golden brown on both sides.
REMOVE from oil. Drain well on paper towelling.
SPRINKLE with mixture of sugar and cinnamon.
SERVE warm or cool.

Carnival Pretzels

Dough:

250 g	all-purpose flour	1⅔ cups
1 pkg	**oetker** instant dry yeast	1 pkg.
25 g	sugar	2 tbsp.
pinch	salt	pinch
1	egg	1
30 g	butter or margarine, melted	2 tbsp.
approx 125 mL	lukewarm milk	½ cup

For deep frying:

oil or shortening

Filling:

250 mL	whipping cream	1 cup
1 pkg	**oetker** Whip-it	1 pkg.
1 pkg	**oetker** vanilla sugar	1 pkg.
30 g	sugar	2 tbsp.

Decoration:

icing sugar, sifted

Dough:

COMBINE flour and yeast in large mixing bowl. Mix well. Make a well in centre.
PUT sugar, salt, egg and melted butter into well.
WORK flour into centre ingredients, gradually addin milk.
KNEAD dough with dough hooks or by hand until smooth, elastic and no longer sticky, about 5 minutes.
COVER with a cloth. Let dough rise in warm place until doubled in size, about 1¼ hours.
KNEAD again.
DIVIDE dough into individual portions, each about 50 g (1¾ oz.).
ROLL into ropes 45 cm (18″) in length.
TWIST into pretzel shapes; see photo.
LET RISE, covered, in warm place, about 20 minute
HEAT oil to 190°C (375°F). Keep at an even temperature.
FRY pretzels, a few at a time, until golden brown on both sides.
REMOVE from oil. Drain well on paper towelling. L cool.
SLICE horizontally into 2 layers.

Filling:

BEAT whipping cream to soft peak. Gradually add Whip-it, vanilla sugar and sugar, beating to stiff peak
PLACE filling onto bottom layers of pretzels using a decorating bag.
COVER with top layers.
SPRINKLE with icing sugar.

Chinese Apple Fritters

Batter:

50 g	all-purpose flour	⅓ cup
1 pkg	**oetker** baking powder	1 pkg.
45 mL	water	3 tbsp.
45 mL	white wine	3 tbsp.
1	egg	1
3	tart apples	3

For deep frying:

oil or shortening

Glaze:

100 g	sugar	½ cup
60 mL	water	¼ cup
5 mL	vinegar	1 tsp.
15 mL	vegetable oil	1 tbsp.

Decoration:

sesame seeds

Batter:

COMBINE flour, baking powder, water, white wine and egg in large mixing bowl. Mix well. Let rest for 10 minutes.
PEEL and core apples, divide each into six wedges. dry.
HEAT oil to 190°C (375°F). Keep at an even temperature.
DIP apple pieces into batter.
FRY, a few at a time, until golden brown on both sides.
REMOVE from oil. Drain well on paper towel.

Glaze:

COMBINE sugar, water and vinegar in saucepan. Bring to a boil.
STIR vegetable oil carefully into mixture. Simmer fo 5-10 minutes.
DIP apple fritters into syrup.
SPRINKLE with sesame seeds.
SERVE warm.

Recipe No. 500 Tunisi

Orange Yo-Yos

Dough:

2	eggs	2
60 mL	vegetable oil	¼ cup
50 g	sugar	¼ cup
60 mL	freshly squeezed orange juice	¼ cup
5 mL	grated orange rind	1 tsp.
300 g	all-purpose flour	2 cups
1 pkg	**oetker** baking powder	1 pkg.

For deep frying:
oil or shortening

Syrup:

500 mL	water	2 cups
½ btl	**oetker** lemon flavouring concentrate	½ btl.
450 g	sugar	2¼ cups
50 mL	liquid honey	3 tbsp.

Batter:
COMBINE eggs and oil in mixer bowl. Beat until light.
BEAT in sugar, orange juice and orange rind gradually.
COMBINE flour and baking powder. Fold into egg mixture, gently but thoroughly.
COVER and let rest 30 minutes.
SHAPE into small balls. Flatten slightly.
CUT small hole in centre of balls.
HEAT oil to 190°C (375°F). Keep at an even temperature.
FRY, a few at a time, until golden brown on both sides.
REMOVE from oil. Drain well on paper towel.
Syrup:
COMBINE water, flavouring concentrate, sugar and honey in saucepan. Bring to a boil, then simmer 5 minutes. Let cool slightly.
POUR over orange yo-yos and serve immediately.

Recipe No. 501 Ital

Grostoi

Dough:

200 g	all-purpose flour	1⅓ cups
5 mL	**oetker** baking powder	1 tsp.
pinch	salt	pinch
1	egg	1
25 g	sugar	2 tbsp.
15 mL	milk	1 tbsp.
45 mL	Grappa or brandy	3 tbsp.
25 g	butter or margarine, cold	2 tbsp.

For deep frying:
oil or shortening

Decoration:
icing sugar, sifted

Dough:
SIFT flour, baking powder and salt onto pastry board
MAKE a well in centre.
PUT egg, sugar, milk and Grappa or brandy in well. Work a little flour into centre mixture to make a stiff dough.
CUT cold butter into small pieces over mixture.
WORK all ingredients together quickly to make a smooth dough.
ROLL out dough very thinly on floured surface.
CUT out 3 cm (1″) squares.
HEAT oil to 190°C (375°F). Keep at an even temperature.
FRY, a few at a time, until golden brown on both sides.
REMOVE from oil. Drain well on paper towel.
SPRINKLE with icing sugar.

Greek Doughnuts with Honey Sauce

Dough:

450	g	all-purpose flour	3 cups
1	pkg	**oetker** instant dry yeast	1 pkg.
25	g	sugar	2 tbsp.
3	mL	salt	½ tsp.
½	btl	**oetker** lemon flavouring concentrate	½ btl.
1		egg	1
375	mL	lukewarm water	1½ cups

For deep frying:

oil or shortening

Sauce:

200	g	sugar	1 cup
200	mL	liquid honey	¾ cup
125	mL	water	½ cup
15	mL	lemon juice	1 tbsp.

Decoration:

30	g	chopped pistachios	¼ cup

Dough:

COMBINE flour and yeast in large mixing bowl. Ma a well in centre.
PUT sugar, salt, flavouring concentrate and egg into well.
WORK flour into centre ingredients, gradually addir water.
KNEAD dough with dough hooks or by hand until smooth, elastic and no longer sticky, about 5 minute
LET RISE, covered, in warm place, about 30 minute
HEAT oil to 190°C (375°F). Keep at an even temperature.
SHAPE balls with tablespoon, dropping dough into hot oil.
FRY a few at a time until golden brown on both sid
REMOVE from oil. Drain well on paper towelling.
KEEP in a warm place.

Sauce:

COMBINE sugar, honey, water and lemon juice in saucepan. Bring to a boil, stirring constantly, then simmer 5 minutes.
POUR hot sauce over doughnuts.
SPRINKLE with pistachios.
SERVE warm.

Baked Bananas

Ingredients:

4		firm bananas, peeled	4
250	mL	white wine or orange juice	1 cup
		all-purpose flour	
75	g	butter or margarine	⅓ cup

Decoration:

2-3	pkg	**oetker** natural vanilla sugar	2-3 pkg.

Method:

PREHEAT oven to 220°C (425°F).
CUT bananas diagonally into 5 mm (¼") slices.
COMBINE banana slices and white wine in saucepa
BRING just to a boil.
REMOVE from heat.
DRAIN bananas well.
TOSS bananas in flour to lightly coat all sides.
HEAT butter in flat baking pan.
PUT bananas in butter in single layer.
SPRINKLE with 1 pkg vanilla sugar.
BROIL, turning once, until golden brown, about 10 minutes.
SPRINKLE with remaining vanilla sugar.
SERVE warm.

SAVOURY BAKING

SPECIALTIES

Calzone

Dough:

400 g	all-purpose flour	2⅔ cups	
1 pkg	**oetker** instant dry yeast	1 pkg.	
3 mL	salt	¾ tsp.	
60 mL	olive oil	¼ cup	
250 mL	lukewarm water	1 cup	

Filling:

	olive oil	
300 g	peeled tomatoes, diced	10 oz.
5 mL	thyme	1 tsp.
250 g	mozzarella cheese, sliced	8 oz.
150 g	onions, sliced into rings	5 oz.
6	fillets of sardines	6
1	egg yolk, slightly beaten	1

Dough:
PREHEAT oven to 200°C (400°F). Grease a baking sheet.
COMBINE flour and yeast in large mixing bowl. Ma a well in centre.
PUT salt, olive oil and water into well.
KNEAD dough with dough hooks or by hand until smooth, elastic and no longer sticky, about 5 minutes
LET rise, covered, in warm place, until doubled in si about 1 hour.
KNEAD again.
DIVIDE into 6 equal portions.
SHAPE into round balls. Press down with hand to about 5 mm (¼″) thick rounds.
BRUSH lightly with olive oil.
Filling:
DISTRIBUTE tomatoes evenly over ½ of each dough round.
SPRINKLE with thyme.
DISTRIBUTE cheese, onions and sardines evenly ov tomatoes.
FOLD dough over filling.
BRUSH edges with water. Press together firmly to se
BRUSH with beaten egg yolk.
PLACE onto prepared baking sheet.
BAKE on middle oven rack at 200°C (400°F) for 20-30 minutes.

Ladiner Bread

Dough:

400 g	all-purpose flour	2⅔ cups
200 g	rye flour	1⅓ cups
2 pkg	**oetker** instant dry yeast	2 pkg.
pinch	sugar	pinch
5 mL	salt	1 tsp.
5 mL	ground coriander	1 tsp.
20 g	linseeds or flax seeds	2 tbsp.
1	egg	1
approx 250 mL	lukewarm milk	1 cup

Glaze:
milk

Decoration:
ground coriander
linseeds or flax seeds

Dough:
PREHEAT oven to 220°C (425°F). Grease a baking sheet.
COMBINE flours and yeast in large mixing bowl. Make a well in centre.
PUT sugar, salt, coriander, linseeds, egg and milk int well.
KNEAD dough with dough hooks or by hand until smooth, elastic and no longer sticky, about 5 minutes
LET rise, covered, in warm place, until doubled in si about 1 hour.
KNEAD again.
DIVIDE into 6 equal portions.
SHAPE into round loaves.
BRUSH with milk.
SPRINKLE with coriander and linseeds.
PLACE onto prepared baking sheet.
BAKE on middle oven rack at 220°C (425°F) for 15-20 minutes.
SERVE warm.

Recipe No. 506 German

Berlin Caraway Rolls

Dough:

500 g	rye flour	3⅓	cups
2 pkg	**oetker** baking powder	2	pkg.
5 mL	salt	1	tsp.
5 mL	caraway seeds	1	tsp.
500 mL	beer	2	cups

Decoration:

1	egg yolk, slightly beaten	1	
	coarse salt		
	caraway seeds		

Dough:

PREHEAT oven to 200°C (400°F). Grease a baking sheet.
SIFT flour and baking powder onto pastry board. Make a well in centre.
PUT salt, caraway seeds and beer into well.
WORK all ingredients together quickly to make a smooth dough.
SHAPE into small rolls.
BRUSH with beaten egg yolk.
SPRINKLE with salt and caraway seeds.
PLACE onto prepared baking sheet.
BAKE on middle oven rack at 200°C (400°F) for 20-30 minutes.

Recipe No. 507 Rus

Perogies

Dough:

250 g	all-purpose flour	1⅔	cups
1 pkg	**oetker** instant dry yeast	1	pkg.
pinch	salt		pinch
1	egg	1	
50 g	shortening	¼	cup
approx 75 mL	lukewarm water	⅓	cup

Filling:

1	onion, finely chopped	1	
250 g	cooked ham, diced	8	oz.
10 g	butter or margarine	1	tbsp.
50 mL	sour cream	3	tbsp.
30 mL	finely chopped parsley	2	tbsp.
	salt, pepper and nutmeg to taste		
1	egg yolk, slightly beaten	1	
30 mL	milk	2	tbsp.

Dough:

PREHEAT oven to 200°C (400°F). Grease a baking sheet.
COMBINE flour and yeast in large mixing bowl. M a well in centre.
PUT salt, egg, shortening and water into well.
KNEAD dough with dough hooks or by hand until smooth, elastic and no longer sticky, about 5 minut
LET rise, covered, in warm place until doubled in si about 1 hour.
KNEAD again.
ROLL out dough on floured surface to 5 mm (¼″) thickness.
CUT out rounds 6 cm (2¼″) in diameter.

Filling:

SAUTE onion and ham in butter until golden.
ADD sour cream.
SEASON with parsley, salt, pepper and nutmeg.
PLACE about 15 mL (1 tbsp.) onto each dough rou
FOLD dough over. Press edges together firmly with fork to seal.
BRUSH with mixture of beaten egg and milk.
PLACE onto prepared baking sheet.
BAKE on middle oven rack at 200°C (400°F) for 20-25 minutes.
SERVE warm.

Recipe No. 508 Switzerla

Onion Quiche

Dough:

Metric	Ingredient	Imperial
300 g	all-purpose flour	2 cups
1 pkg	**oetker** instant dry yeast	1 pkg.
pinch	salt	pinch
1	egg	1
60 g	butter or margarine, melted	⅓ cup
approx 125 mL	lukewarm milk	½ cup

Filling:

Metric	Ingredient	Imperial
1 kg	onions, chopped	2 lbs.
125 g	bacon, diced	4 oz.
125 mL	whipping cream	½ cup
4	eggs	4
	salt, pepper and nutmeg to taste	
12	slices bacon, partially cooked	12

Dough:

PREHEAT oven to 200°C (400°F). Grease a 24 cm (9½″) springform pan.
COMBINE flour and yeast in large mixing bowl. Ma a well in centre.
PUT salt, egg, melted butter and milk into well.
KNEAD dough with dough hooks or by hand until smooth, elastic and no longer sticky, about 5 minutes
LET RISE, covered, in warm place until doubled in size, about 1 hour.
KNEAD again.
PRESS dough evenly onto bottom and 4 cm (1½″) u sides of prepared pan.

Filling:

SAUTE onions and bacon until golden. Cool slightly
SPREAD evenly onto dough.
COMBINE whipping cream, eggs, salt, pepper and nutmeg. Mix well.
POUR evenly over onion mixture.
BAKE on middle oven rack at 200°C (400°F) for 20-30 minutes.
DECORATE with bacon slices.
BAKE 5 minutes longer.

Recipe No. 509 Yugoslav

Baltic Onion Buns

Dough:

Metric	Ingredient	Imperial
300 g	all-purpose flour	2 cups
1 pkg	**oetker** instant dry yeast	1 pkg.
pinch	salt	pinch
1	egg	1
60 g	butter or margarine, melted	⅓ cup
approx 125 mL	lukewarm milk	½ cup

Filling:

Metric	Ingredient	Imperial
40 g	onions, finely chopped	1 oz.
125 g	smoked bacon, diced	4 oz.
20 g	shortening	2 tbsp.
	salt, pepper and caraway seeds to taste	
1	egg yolk, slightly beaten	1
15 mL	milk	1 tbsp.

Dough:

PREHEAT oven to 220°C (425°F). Grease a baking sheet.
COMBINE flour and yeast in large mixing bowl. Ma a well in centre.
PUT salt, egg, melted butter and milk into well.
KNEAD dough with dough hooks or by hand until smooth, elastic and no longer sticky, about 5 minutes
LET RISE, covered, in warm place until doubled in size, about 40 minutes.
KNEAD again.
DIVIDE into 8 portions. Press each dough round wi hand to flatten.

Filling:

SAUTE onions and bacon in shortening until golden
SEASON to taste with salt, pepper and caraway seed
PLACE about 15 mL (1 tbsp.) onto each dough roun
FOLD dough over, shaping into rolls. Press edges together firmly to seal.
LET RISE 15 minutes.
PLACE onto prepared baking sheet.
BRUSH with mixture of beaten egg yolk and milk.
BAKE on middle oven rack at 220°C (425°F) for 12-15 minutes.

Recipe No. 510 Gre

Greek Rolls

Dough:

3 mL	sea salt	¾	tsp.
250 mL	lukewarm water	1	cup
350 g	all-purpose flour	2⅓	cups
1 pkg	**oetker** instant dry yeast	1	pkg.
15 mL	olive oil	1	tbsp.

Filling:

200 g	goat cheese (chevre)	7	oz.
2	eggs, slightly beaten	2	
10 mL	finely chopped mint	2	tsp.
pinch	pepper		pinch
50 g	butter or margarine, melted	¼	cup

Dough:
PREHEAT oven to 200°C (400°F). Grease a bakin sheet.
DISSOLVE sea salt in a little hot water. Mix with 250 mL (1 cup) lukewarm water.
COMBINE flour and yeast in large mixing bowl. M a well in centre.
PUT water mixture and olive oil into well.
KNEAD dough with dough hooks or by hand until smooth, elastic and no longer sticky, about 5 minut
LET RISE, covered, in warm place until doubled in size, about 1½ hours.
KNEAD again.
DIVIDE into 8 portions.
SHAPE into 8 rounds.
PINCH up edges.
PLACE onto prepared baking sheet.
Filling:
COMBINE cheese, eggs, mint and pepper. Mix well
SPREAD filling evenly over 8 dough rounds.
BAKE on middle oven rack at 200°C (400°F) for 10-15 minutes.
REDUCE heat to 180°C (350°F) and bake 10-15 minutes longer.
BRUSH with melted butter.
SERVE hot.

Recipe No. 511 Switzerla

Basler Snacks

Dough:

500 g	all-purpose flour	3⅓	cups
1 pkg	**oetker** instant dry yeast	1	pkg.
pinch	salt		pinch
pinch	sugar		pinch
150 g	butter or margarine, melted	¾	cup
approx 250 mL	lukewarm milk	1	cup
1	egg yolk, slightly beaten	1	
	caraway seeds		

Dough:
PREHEAT oven to 225°C (450°F). Grease a baking sheet.
COMBINE flour and yeast in large mixing bowl. M a well in centre.
PUT salt, sugar, melted butter and milk into well.
KNEAD dough with dough hooks or by hand until smooth, elastic and no longer sticky, about 5 minute
LET RISE, covered, in warm place until doubled in size, about 1 hour.
KNEAD again.
ROLL out dough on floured surface to 5 mm (¼") thickness.
CUT out shapes of Basler town emblem; see photo.
PLACE onto prepared baking sheet.
BRUSH with beaten egg yolk.
SPRINKLE with caraway seeds.
BAKE on middle oven rack at 225°C (450°F) for 5-10 minutes.

BASILEA

Recipe No. 512 | Fra

Quiche Lorraine

Pastry:

130 g	all-purpose flour	1	cup
5 mL	**oetker** baking powder	1	tsp.
1	egg	1	
pinch	salt		pinch
80 g	butter or margarine, cold	⅓	cup

Filling:

150 g	cooked ham, diced	5	oz.
200 g	grated Swiss or Emmental cheese	7	oz.
2	eggs	2	
250 mL	sour cream	1	cup
2 mL	salt	½	tsp.
1 mL	nutmeg	¼	tsp.
1 mL	pepper	¼	tsp.
1 mL	paprika	¼	tsp.

Pastry:
PREHEAT oven to 180°C (350°F). Grease a 24 cm (9½″) springform pan or quiche pan.
SIFT flour and baking powder onto pastry board. Make a well in centre.
PUT egg and salt in well. Work a little flour into centre mixture to make a stiff dough.
CUT cold butter into small pieces over mixture.
WORK all ingredients together quickly to make a smooth dough.
PRESS or roll ⅔ of pastry onto bottom of prepared pan. Trim to fit.
SHAPE remaining pastry into a long roll. Press arc inside rim of pan forming 4 cm (1½″) sides. Press seams to seal.
Filling:
SPRINKLE ham and cheese evenly over pastry.
COMBINE eggs, sour cream, salt, nutmeg, pepper paprika. Mix well.
POUR evenly over ham and cheese.
BAKE on bottom oven rack at 180°C (350°F) for 30-35 minutes.
SERVE warm.

Recipe No. 513 | Bulga

Banitsa

Pastry:

2 pkg	frozen puff pastry (397 g/14 oz. each)	2	pkg.

Filling:

250 g	goat cheese (chevre)	8	oz.
2	eggs	2	
125 mL	plain yogurt	½	cup
125 mL	sour cream	½	cup

Glaze:

1	egg, slightly beaten	1	

Batter:
PREHEAT oven to 200°C (400°F). Grease a bakin sheet.
THAW puff pastry according to package directions
ROLL out pastry very thinly.
CUT into 10 × 20 cm (4″ × 8″) rectangles.
STRAIN cheese through a sieve.
COMBINE cheese, eggs, yogurt and sour cream. M well.
FILL into a decorating bag and squeeze evenly ont pastry rectangles OR spread filling onto pastry with knife.
ROLL up dough starting at longer side.
SHAPE into desired S-shapes on prepared baking sheet.
BRUSH with beaten egg.
BAKE on middle oven rack at 200°C (400°F) for 15-20 minutes.
SERVE warm.

oetker Baking Powder
Baked goods obtain a light and tender, fine, even texture, **oetker** Baking Powder leaves no after taste. Individual, premeasured, coated and tightly sealed pouches guarantee freshness and success every time.

oetker Vanilla Sugar
It blends instantly and uniformly in dry as well as liquid ingredients. There is no colour change with the **oetker** product as there is with the brown liquid vanilla. No measuring required – just sprinkle.

oetker Natural Vanilla Sugar
Is produced from the extract of vanilla beans. It has the true rich, smooth, full taste that your baking deserves.

oetker Instant Dry Yeast
Requires no refrigeration. It is mixed directly with the flour, eliminating the pre-mixing with liquid step. Its increased rising power will also save time.

oetker Whip it
Keeps whipped cream stiff and appetizing for hours. **Whip it** is completely neutral in colour and taste.

oetker Glaze (clear and red)
Is easy to prepare and sets fast. Its sparkling clear appearance enhances and preserves the colour, flavour and freshness of fruit flans.

oetker Chocofix
Is a beautiful chocolate frosting and glaze that is extremely quick, easy and convenient to prepare. The foil pouch is softened in boiling water then poured directly onto your cake dessert. Dutch cocoa powder gives **Chocofix** its unique full, rich European chocolate flavour.

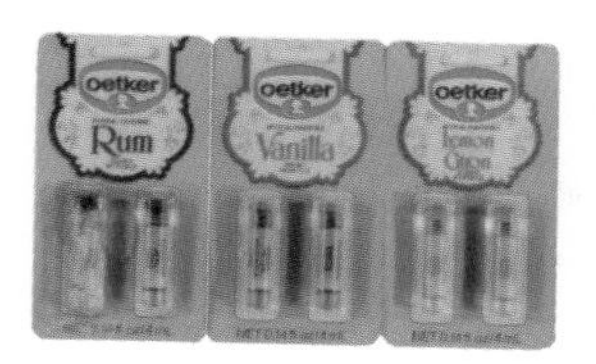

oetker Flavouring Concentrates
Retain the true, natural flavour and aroma during baking. They are easy and convenient to use and are four times more concentrated than regular flavourings.

Langnese Honey
For recipes with honey we recommend Langnese Honey. It is a natural, pure product. Use Langnese Honey to sweeten hot or cold drinks, cereal, fruit, pancakes and waffles.

oetker Vanilla Sauce
Whether omelette, chocolate pudding, jelly or fresh fruit – everything tastes better with **oetker Vanilla Sauce.** Easy to prepare.

oetker Gelatine
Sparkling, clear gelatine will make a success of fish, meat and vegetable dishes in aspic. Use it also in sweet dishes, jellies and as a glaze for fruit flans.

oetker Gustin
Is a fine food starch used for baking; cakes, cookies and pastries will be light, fluffy and have a nicer texture. Gustin also thickens soups and sauces smoothly.

oetker Instant Glaze – Fruit and Strawberry
Both glazes are presweetened and give a nice, shiny appearance to fruit pies. Easy to prepare – just add boiling water. Fruit glaze is crystal clear and unflavoured. Strawberry glaze is red in colour and naturally flavoured.

Notes

Notes

Notes